AMERICAN
WAR LIBRARY

★ World War II ★

PRIMARY SOURCES

Edited by David M. Haugen

LUCENT
BOOKS®

THOMSON
★
GALE

San Diego • Detroit • New York • San Francisco • Cleveland • New Haven, Conn. • Waterville, Maine • London • Munich

LIBRARY OF CONGRESS CATALOGING-IN-PUBLICATION DATA

World War II : primary sources / [edited] by David M. Haugen.
    p. cm. — (American war library. World War II)
Summary: Presents the original documents used as source material for the
American War Library, World War II series, including works by FDR, Eisenhower,
Truman, Hersey, Steinbeck, Murrow, and Pyle.
Includes bibliographical references and index.
    ISBN 1-59018-204-9 (hardback : alk. paper)
  1. World War, 1939–1945—Sources—Juvenile literature. [1. World War,
1939–1945—Sources.] I. Title: World War 2. II. Title: World War Two.
III. Haugen, David M., 1969– IV. Series.
    D735 .W66 2003
    940.53—dc21
                                                                2002003817

✫ Contents ✫

A Nation Forged by War

The United States, like many nations, was forged and defined by war. Despite Benjamin Franklin's opinion that "There never was a good war or a bad peace," the United States owes its very existence to the War of Independence, one to which Franklin wholeheartedly subscribed. The country forged by war in 1776 was tempered and made stronger by the Civil War in the 1860s.

The Texas Revolution, the Mexican-American War, and the Spanish-American War expanded the country's borders and gave it overseas possessions. These wars made the United States a world power, but this status came with a price, as the nation became a key but reluctant player in both World War I and World War II.

Each successive war further defined the country's role on the world stage. Following World War II, U.S. foreign policy redefined itself to focus on the role of defender, not only of the freedom of its own citizens, but also of the freedom of

people everywhere. During the cold war that followed World War II until the collapse of the Soviet Union, defending the world meant fighting communism. This goal, manifested in the Korean and Vietnam conflicts, proved elusive, and soured the American public on its achievability. As the United States emerged as the world's sole superpower, American foreign policy has been guided less by national interest and more on protecting international human rights. But as involvement in Somalia and Kosovo prove, this goal has been equally elusive.

As a result, the country's view of itself changed. Bolstered by victories in World Wars I and II, Americans first relished the role of protector. But, as war followed war in a seemingly endless procession, Americans began to doubt their leaders, their motives, and themselves. The Vietnam War especially caused people to question the validity of sending its young people to die in places where they were not particularly wanted and for people who did not seem especially grateful.

While the most obvious changes brought about by America's wars have been geopolitical in nature, many other aspects of society have been touched. War often does not bring about change directly, but acts instead like the catalyst in a chemical reaction, accelerating changes already in progress.

Some of these changes have been societal. The role of women in the United States had been slowly changing, but World War II put thousands into the workforce and into uniform. They might have gone back to being housewives after the war, but equality, once experienced, would not be forgotten.

Likewise, wars have accelerated technological change. The necessity for faster airplanes and a more destructive bomb led to the development of jet planes and nuclear energy. Artificial fibers developed for parachutes in the 1940s were used in the clothing of the 1950s.

Lucent Books' American War Library covers key wars in the development of the nation. Each war is covered in several volumes, to allow for more detail and context, and to provide volumes on often neglected subjects, such as the kamikazes of World War II, or weapons used in the Civil War. As with all Lucent Books, notes, annotated bibliographies, and appendixes such as glossaries give students a launching point for further research. In addition, sidebars and archival photographs enhance the text. Together, each volume in The American War Library will aid students in understanding how America's wars have shaped and changed its politics, economics, and society.

Chapter 1

The End of Isolation

When World War II began in Europe in September 1939, the United States was content to let the conflict remain a European affair. America had helped fight the previous world war and had little to show for it except thousands of dead soldiers. Isolationists, those who were strongly opposed to America's involvement in foreign affairs, argued that the nation should tend to its own problems. The United States, after all, was still suffering the ills of the Great Depression. People had a difficult time making ends meet and little incentive to involve themselves in a war across the sea where tyrants and monarchs had a history of squabbling with their neighbors.

Many Americans agreed with the isolationists in the years between the two world wars. In 1936, Congress had passed a law to make loans to any belligerent or warring nation illegal. And when the Spanish Civil War erupted in that same year, the law was extended to prevent the United States from supplying aid of any kind to either side of a conflict. The isolationists in government were determined not to let the United States get dragged into another foreign war.

Despite the convincing arguments of some congressmen, not all government officials favored American neutrality. Those who encouraged intervening in the European war pointed out that the fascist dictators of Germany, Italy, and Spain were bent on subjugating Europe and would probably not be content to end their conquest at European shores. Besides, if the Nazi regime and its allies were successful in their endeavors, the world would resemble an armed camp and America would have to compete to maintain a military edge on would-be aggressors or risk being conquered itself. These interventionists wanted to aid the Allies—mainly Britain and France—to ensure the future safety of the United States and the world at large.

Most American citizens were torn by these two competing agendas. Many had sympathy for the Allied cause but were still hesitant to offer up American blood for a European struggle. President Franklin D. Roosevelt, sensing the mood of the nation, called Congress into a special session to amend the Neutrality Act, which was designed to prevent the United States from taking sides in foreign wars. The new legislation would allow America to sell arms and other supplies to the Allied nations on a "cash and carry" basis—meaning as long as the nations paid for the weapons, the United States would supply them. Isolation-

German soldiers ride through Poland after their 1939 invasion.

ists protested, noting that the country could not maintain neutrality and support the Allies. But the warnings of the interventionists were more compelling.

In June of 1940, France surrendered to the Nazi armies that had stormed across its borders. Now, only England stood against the might of the fascist nations. Without help, it seemed certain that the tiny island nation would eventually succumb. Roosevelt began preparing the United States for war. He instituted a draft to increase the size of the miniscule U.S. military. He also began "lending" Britain armaments on a lease program that involved deferred payment. The "Lend-Lease" initiative helped financially strapped Britain gain tanks, ships, and airplanes to continue the fight.

These actions did not unite the country behind the Allied war effort. Congress was still divided on the issue, and barely a quarter of U.S. citizens supported American involvement. The president wisely refrained from prompting Congress into a declaration of war. But other forces were at work that would eventually compel the United States to take its stand against tyranny.

Although not as successful as the larger nations, the Japanese empire had been trying its hand at conquest in Asia while the Germans and Italians were marching through Europe and Africa. In the early 1930s, Japan had taken Manchuria from China and then trumped up reasons to invade China proper. President Roosevelt was very wary of Japanese militarism because the United States had many territories in the Pacific that would be useful to the em-

An American paperboy sells newspapers reporting the Japanese attack on Pearl Harbor.

pire. He warned the Japanese emperor not to threaten U.S. interests but he really had no power to enforce his words. However, the war in Europe was also demanding his attention. Japan seized on the moment and launched a surprise raid against the American naval installation at Pearl Harbor, Hawaii, on December 7, 1941. America was now at war with the Japanese. And, since

Japan had joined the Axis league of nations that included Germany and Italy, the fascists supported their ally. On December 10, Adolf Hitler and the Nazi state declared war on the United States. Dissenting voices in the United States were quelled almost immediately. Neutrality was no longer an issue as Americans geared up to fight another world war.

The United States Should Remain Neutral

Two days after Hitler's armies invaded neighboring Poland, President Franklin D. Roosevelt addressed the American public in one of his many radio broadcasts. Roosevelt had begun speaking over the radio during the Great Depression to calm public fears and explain government strategies. Roosevelt's broadcasts had come to be known as "fireside chats" because of their informal character and the fact that they were transmitted directly into people's homes where whole families could gather and listen. The goal of Roosevelt's broadcast on September 3 was no different than previous ones. With the outbreak of hostilities in Europe, many Americans were concerned that they would be dragged into another world war. Although sections of the public were in favor of backing France, Britain, and the other Allied forces, Roosevelt spoke of maintaining America's neutrality. According to the president, after World War I, American policy was to adopt a neutral stance in world affairs and to always promote peace. Roosevelt avowed that he would enforce those principles and would do everything in his power to stop war from spreading to the Americas.

Tonight my single duty is to speak to the whole of America. Until four-thirty this morning I had hoped against hope that some miracle would prevent a devastating war in Europe and bring to an end the invasion of Poland by Germany.

For four long years a succession of actual wars and constant crises have shaken the entire world and have threatened in each case to bring on the gigantic conflict which is today unhappily a fact.

It is right that I should recall to your minds the consistent and at times successful efforts of your Government in these crises to throw the full weight of the United States into the cause of peace. In spite of spreading wars I think that we have every right and every reason to maintain as a national policy the fundamental moralities, the teachings of religion, and the continuation of efforts to restore peace—for some day, though the time may be distant, we can be of even greater help to a crippled humanity. . . .

It is, of course, impossible to predict the future. I have my constant stream of information from American representatives and other sources throughout the world. You, the people of this country, are receiving news through your radios and your newspapers at every hour of the day.

You are, I believe, the most enlightened and the best informed people in all the world at this moment. You are subjected to no censorship of news, and I want to add that your Government has no information which it withholds or which it has any thought of withholding from you.

At the same time, as I told my press conference on Friday, it is of the highest importance that the press and the radio use the utmost caution to discriminate between actual verified fact on the one hand, and mere rumor on the other. . . .

Let no man or woman thoughtlessly or falsely talk of America sending its armies to European fields. At this moment there is being prepared a proclamation of American neutrality. This would have been done even if there had been no neutrality statute on the books, for this proclamation is in accordance with international law and in accordance with American policy.

This will be followed by a Proclamation required by the existing Neutrality Act. And I trust that in the days to come our neutrality can be made a true neutrality.

It is of the utmost importance that the people of this country, with the best information in the world, think things through. The most dangerous enemies of American peace are those who, without well-rounded information on the whole broad subject of the past, the present and the future, undertake to speak with assumed authority, to talk in terms of glittering generalities, to give to the nation assurances or prophesies which are of little present or future value.

I myself cannot and do not prophesy the course of events abroad—and the reason is that, because I have of necessity such a complete picture of what is going on in every part of the world, I do not dare to do so. And the other reason is that I think it is honest for me to be honest with the people of the United States.

I cannot prophesy the immediate economic effect of this new war on our nation, but I do say that no American has the moral right to profiteer at the expense either of his fellow citizens or of the men, the women and the children who are living and dying in the midst of war in Europe.

Some things we do know. Most of us in the United States believe in spiritual values. Most of us, regardless of what church we belong to, believe in the spirit of the New Testament—a great teaching which opposes itself to the use of force, of armed force, of marching armies and falling bombs. The overwhelming masses of our people seek peace—peace at home, and the kind of peace in other lands which will not jeopardize our peace at home.

We have certain ideas and certain ideals of national safety, and we must act to preserve that safety today, and to preserve the safety of our children in future years.

That safety is and will be bound up with the safety of the Western Hemisphere and of the seas adjacent thereto. We seek to keep war from our own firesides by keeping war from coming to the Americas. For that we have historic precedent that goes back to the days of the Administration of President George Washington. It is serious enough and tragic enough to every American family in every State in the Union to live in a world that is torn by wars on other continents. Those wars today affect every American home. It is our national duty to use every effort to keep them out of the Americas.

And at this time let me make the simple plea that partisanship and selfishness be adjourned; and that national unity be the thought that underlies all others.

This Nation will remain a neutral Nation, but I cannot ask that every American remain neutral in thought as well. Even a neutral has a right to take account of facts. Even a neutral cannot be asked to close his mind or his conscience.

I have said not once, but many times, that I have seen war and that I hate war. I say that again and again.

I hope the United States will keep out of this war. I believe that it will. And I give you assurance and reassurance that every effort of your Government will be directed toward that end.

As long as it remains within my power to prevent, there will be no black-out of peace in the United States.

Excerpted from Franklin D. Roosevelt's "Fireside Chat" radio broadcast, September 3, 1939.

The Dangers of Breaking Neutrality

On September 21, 1939, President Roosevelt called Congress into session to revise America's neutrality laws. The revision was to include a relaxing of the nation's ban on selling weapons to warring nations. Many isolationists in America perceived this as a dangerous risk that would draw the United States into the conflict. In fact, many of these antiwar advocates believed the president was scheming to sell weapons to the Allies to eventually maneuver America into backing their cause. A Republican senator from Michigan, Arthur H. Vandenberg, was one isolationist who spoke out against amending the nation's neutrality laws. Although not accusing Roosevelt of wrongdoing, Vandenberg speaks of the costs of America's involvement in the First World War and the consequences of becoming entangled in yet another foreign war. Vandenberg and the other isolationists won a temporary victory as Congress ultimately did not adopt the president's proposed changes.

Mr. President, I believe this debate symbolically involves the most momentous decision, in the eyes of America and of the world, that the United States Senate has confronted in a generation. In the midst of foreign war and the alarms of other wars, we are asked to depart basically from the neutrality which the American Congress has twice told the world, since 1935, would be our rule of conduct in such event. We are particularly asked to depart from it through the repeal of existing neutrality law establishing an embargo on arms, ammunition, and implements of war. We are asked to depart from it in violation of our own officially asserted doctrine, during the [first] World War, that the rules of a neutral cannot be prejudicially altered in the midst of a war. We are asked to depart from international law itself, as we ourselves have officially declared it to exist. Consciously or otherwise, but mostly consciously, we are asked to depart from it in behalf of one belligerent whom our personal sympathies largely favor, and against another belligerent whom our personal feelings largely condemn. In my opinion, this is the road that may lead us to war, and I will not voluntarily take it. . . .

To those Americans who are not too unwilling to believe it may be necessary or wise for us not only to scrap the arms embargo, but even to go further in support of one belligerent today against the other, I ask, what would we, what could we get out of participation in this new war, even on the assured presumption that we would emerge victorious? What would we get?

First, we would get such a regimentation of our own lives and livelihoods, 20 minutes after we entered the war, that the Bill of Rights would need a gas mask, and individual liberty of action would swiftly become a mocking memory. This is not hyperbole. Scan the Army's industrial mobilization plan, for example. We have previewed it here in Congress. I quote a few typical sentences from a recent authentic newspaper review:

> Labor and business would be regimented. . . . Strikes would be outlawed. . . . Employers would be told by Government what wages to pay and hours to work; what prices to charge; what profits to make. . . . The Government would dictate costs, prices, interest rates, rents, etc. . . . Light, heat, food will be rationed—

And so forth. Another columnist says:

> It is the complete disappearance of an individual's or a corporation's liberty of choice and action—social and economic—which reveals how closely the United States will resemble a Fascist country controlled by a Mussolini or a Hitler.

Let no one distort what I am saying. Specifically I am not charging, even by remotest inference, that this administration has some malignant purpose to chain our freedom through its abuse of war powers. I am simply saying that these chains are inherent in the new war technique all around the globe, and that our own official expectations, in some quarters, anticipate this mold. . . .

Second, we should come out of the victory with an infinitely pyramided debt. If the war dragged on, the debt would not be long in staggering toward $100,000,000,000. It never could be carried or repaid. Repudiation or ruinous inflation would be inevitable. Our economic values would collapse. Nothing but all-powerful central government could save the pieces. We should ultimately understand what old King Pyrrhus meant when he said, "Another such victory and we are lost." We should win another war and lose another peace. Nobody can win anything else.

Discount as you please, Mr. President, this prospectus and its dread casualty rolls, nevertheless, it approximates the outline of our destiny in some degree if we go to Europe to fight another European war. . . .

It is entirely human—and a credit to our sensibilities—to give vent to our outraged emotions from time to time in the presence of broken liberties and broken lives beneath other flags. But surely our paramount responsibility—every minute of every hour in every day—is so to maintain our national attitudes that the wars of others do not needlessly come to us, and that whatever destruction happens elsewhere may not needlessly happen here. This is not our war. We did not start it. We have no control over its course. We cannot dictate its conclusion. We cannot order Europe's destiny, not even if we took it as a permanent assignment. It is not our war, despite our devotion to democracy. It need not—it should not—become our war. We should deliberately and consciously stay all the way out unless and until we are deliberately and consciously ready to go all the way in. . . .

If we ever reach the point where the American people are substantially convinced that American destiny is unavoidably dependent upon and inseverably linked with the fate of one side or the other in a European war—which, in spite of my predilections, I strongly deny—or if we ever find one of these belligerents invading essential democracy in the United States or in this Western World, then let us not be content merely to edge our way toward war in the disguise of a neutral, but let us go all the way in with everything we have got. But God forbid the arrival of such a zero hour. Meanwhile, let us stay all the way out.

Excerpted from *Congressional Record*, by Arthur H. Vandenberg, 76th Cong., 2nd Sess., October 4, 1939.

The Dire Situation in London

While the United States remained neutral, war raged in Europe. By late 1940, the Nazi blitzkrieg had conquered Poland, the Low Countries (Belgium, Holland, and Luxembourg), and France, leaving England the sole Allied power to oppose the German juggernaut. England's situation looked dire, as Hitler ordered bombings on Britain's cities and even contemplated a seaborne invasion of the island nation. Although London was subjected to numerous bombings and parts of the city were leveled, the English would not surrender.

Edward R. Murrow was a CBS radio newsman who broadcast the events from London to an anxious American public. Murrow's reports conveyed the brutality of the German raids and the spirited perseverance of the English people. The drama of the London Blitz helped sway public opinion in America and made Britain and the Allies appear as the underdogs in a fight against tyranny and evil.

October 10, 1940

This is London, ten minutes before five in the morning. Tonight's raid has been widespread. London is again the main target. Bombs have been reported from more than fifty districts. Raiders have been over Wales in the west, the Midlands, Liverpool, the southwest, and northeast. So far as London is concerned, the outskirts appear to have suffered the heaviest pounding. The attack has decreased in intensity since the moon faded from the sky.

All the fires were quickly brought under control. That's a common phrase in the morning communiqués. I've seen how it's done; spent a night with the London fire brigade. For three hours after the night attack got going, I shivered in a sandbag crow's-nest atop a tall building near the Thames. It was one of the many fire-observation posts. There was an old gun barrel mounted above a round table marked off like a compass. A stick of incendiaries [explosive materials] bounced off rooftops about three miles away. The observer took a sight on a point where the first one fell, swung his gun sight along the line of bombs, and took another reading at the end of the line of fire. Then he picked up his telephone and shouted above the half gale that was blowing up there, "Stick of incendiaries—between 190 and 220—about three miles away." Five minutes later a German bomber came boring down the river. We could see his exhaust trail like a pale ribbon stretched straight across the sky. Half a mile downstream there were two eruptions and then a third, close together. The first two looked like some giant had thrown a huge basket of flaming golden oranges high in the air. The third was just a balloon of fire enclosed in black smoke above the housetops. The observer didn't bother with his gun sight and indicator for that one. Just reached for his night glasses, took one quick look, picked up his telephone, and said, "Two high explosives and one oil bomb," and named the street where they had fallen. . . .

There was peace and quiet inside for twenty minutes. Then a shower of incendiaries came down far in the distance. . . . Half an hour later a string of fire bombs fell right beside the Thames. Their white glare was reflected in the black, lazy water near the banks and faded out in midstream where the moon cut a golden swathe broken only by the arches of famous bridges.

Radio broadcaster Edward R. Murrow reports from London during the 1940 Nazi air attack on the city.

We could see little men shoveling those fire bombs into the river. One burned for a few minutes like a beacon right in the middle of a bridge. Finally those white flames all went out. No one bothers about the white light, it's only when it turns yellow that a real fire has started.

I must have seen well over a hundred fire bombs come down and only three small

The dome of St. Paul's Cathedral in London stands amidst tumbling buildings destroyed by Nazi air raids.

fires were started. The incendiaries aren't so bad if there is someone there to deal with them, but those oil bombs present more difficulties.

As I watched those white fires flame up and die down, watched the yellow blazes grow dull and disappear, I thought, what a puny effort is this to burn a great city. Finally, we went below to a big room underground. It was quiet. Women spoke softly into telephones. There was a big map of London on the wall. Little colored pins were being moved from one point to another and every time a pin was moved it meant that fire pumps were on their way through the black streets of London to a fire. One district had asked for reinforcements from another, just as an army reinforces its front lines in the sector bearing the brunt of the attack. On another map all the observation posts, like the one I just left, were marked. . . .

We picked a fire from the map and drove to it. And the map was right. It was a small fire in a warehouse near the river. Not much of a fire; only ten pumps working on it, but still big enough to be seen from the air. The searchlights were bunched overhead and as we approached we could hear the drone of a German plane and see the burst of antiaircraft fire directly overhead. Two pieces of shrapnel slapped down in the water and then everything was drowned in the hum of the pumps and the sound of hissing water. Those firemen in their oilskins and tin hats appeared oblivious to everything but the fire. We went to another blaze—just a small two-story house down on the East End.

An incendiary had gone through the roof and the place was being gutted. A woman stood on a corner, clutching a rather dirty pillow. A policeman was trying to comfort her. And a fireman said, "You'd be surprised what strange things people pick up when they run out of a burning house."

And back at headquarters I saw a man laboriously and carefully copying names in a big ledger—the list of firemen killed in action during the last month. There were about a hundred names.

Excerpted from Edward R. Murrow's CBS news broadcast, September 10 and October 10, 1940. Copyright © 1940 by Central Broadcasting System. Reprinted with permission.

The United States Should Aid the Allies

After the fall of France in 1940, the United States began actively supporting the Allied war effort. Although the nation was officially neutral, President Franklin D. Roosevelt found ways to circumvent the laws that forbade America from supplying the Allies with any war materials that they could not immediately pay for. Britain was strapped for cash but desperately in need of U.S. supplies, so Roosevelt and his advisers came up with a policy called "Lend-Lease" in which the United States could provide aid to nations that were deemed vital to America's own security. Under Lend-Lease, the Allies could receive goods now but not pay for them until after the war.

Isolationists saw through Roosevelt's pro-Allied policy and warned that such aid would eventually lead to the sending of American sol-diers to fight in European battlefields. To counter his vocal opponents and pacify public fears, Roosevelt staged another radio "fireside chat" on December 29, 1940, to explain his motives. He argued that America had to become "the great arsenal of democracy" in order to protect its own interests and oppose the forces of tyranny that would eventually seek to subjugate the nation. A few days later on January 6, 1941, Roosevelt addressed Congress and again put forth the notion that America was simply acting in its own best interests and in the interests of preserving democracy worldwide. It is in this speech before Congress that the president first laid out the "four freedoms" that America was willing to defend at any cost.

Every realist knows that the democratic way of life is at this moment being directly assailed in every part of the world—assailed either by arms or by secret spreading of poisonous propaganda by those who seek to destroy unity and promote discord in nations still at peace.

During 16 months this assault has blotted out the whole pattern of democratic life in an appalling number of independent nations, great and small. The assailants are still on the march, threatening other nations, great and small.

Therefore, as your President, performing my constitutional duty to "give to the Congress information of the state of the Union," I find it necessary to report that the future and the safety of our country and of our democracy are overwhelmingly involved in events far beyond our borders.

Armed defense of democratic existence is now being gallantly waged in four continents. If that defense fails, all the population and all the resources of Europe, Asia, Africa, and Australasia will be dominated by the conquerors. The total of those populations and their resources greatly exceeds the sum total of the population and resources of the whole of the Western Hemisphere—many times over.

In times like these it is immature—and incidentally untrue—for anybody to brag that an unprepared America, single-handed, and with one hand tied behind its back, can hold off the whole world.

No realistic American can expect from a dictator's peace international generosity, or return of true independence, or world disarmament, or freedom of expression, or freedom of religion—or even good business.

Such a peace would bring no security for us or for our neighbors. "Those who would give up essential liberty to purchase a little temporary safety deserve neither liberty nor safety." . . .

The need of the moment is that our actions and our policy should be devoted primarily—almost exclusively—to meeting this foreign peril. For all our domestic problems are now a part of the great emergency.

Just as our national policy in internal affairs has been based upon a decent respect for the rights and dignity of all our fellowmen within our gates, so our national policy in foreign affairs has been based on a decent respect for the rights and dignity of all

nations, large and small. And the justice of morality must and will win in the end. . . .

I . . . ask this Congress for authority and for funds sufficient to manufacture additional munitions and war supplies of many kinds, to be turned over to those nations which are now in actual war with aggressor nations.

Our most useful and immediate role is to act as an arsenal for them as well as for ourselves. They do not need manpower. They do need billions of dollars' worth of the weapons of defense.

The time is near when they will not be able to pay for them in ready cash. We cannot, and will not, tell them they must surrender merely because of present inability to pay for the weapons which we know they must have.

I do not recommend that we make them a loan of dollars with which to pay for these weapons—a loan to be repaid in dollars.

I recommend that we make it possible for those nations to continue to obtain war materials in the United States, fitting their orders into our own program. Nearly all of their matériel would, if the time ever came, be useful for our own defense.

Taking counsel of expert military and naval authorities, considering what is best for our own security, we are free to decide how much should be kept here and how much should be sent abroad to our friends who, by their determined and heroic resistance, are giving us time in which to make ready our own defense.

For what we send abroad we shall be repaid, within a reasonable time following the close of hostilities, in similar materials or, at our option, in other goods of many kinds which they can produce and which we need.

Let us say to the democracies, "We Americans are vitally concerned in your defense of freedom. We are putting forth our energies, our resources, and our organizing powers to give you the strength to regain and maintain a free world. We shall send you, in ever-increasing numbers, ships, planes, tanks, guns. This is our purpose and our pledge."

In fulfillment of this purpose we will not be intimidated by the threats of dictators that they will regard as a breach of international law and as an act of war our aid to the democracies which dare to resist their aggression. Such aid is not an act of war, even if a dictator should unilaterally proclaim it so to be.

When the dictators are ready to make war upon us, they will not wait for an act of war on our part. They did not wait for Norway or Belgium or the Netherlands to commit an act of war.

Their only interest is in a new one-way international law, which lacks mutuality in its observance and, therefore, becomes an instrument of oppression. . . .

In the future days, which we seek to make secure, we look forward to a world founded upon four essential human freedoms.

The first is freedom of speech and expression everywhere in the world.

The second is freedom of every person to worship God in his own way everywhere in the world.

The third is freedom from want, which, translated into world terms, means economic understandings which will secure to every nation a healthy peacetime life for its inhabitants everywhere in the world.

The fourth is freedom from fear—which, translated into world terms, means a world-wide reduction of armaments to such a point and in such a thorough fashion that no nation will be in a position to commit an act of physical aggression against any neighbor—anywhere in the world.

That is no vision of a distant millennium. It is a definite basis for a kind of world attainable in our own time and generation. That kind of world is the very antithesis of the so-called new order of tyranny which the dictators seek to create with the crash of a bomb.

To that new order we oppose the greater conception—the moral order. A good society is able to face schemes of world domination and foreign revolutions alike without fear. . . .

This Nation has placed its destiny in the hands and heads and hearts of its millions of free men and women; and its faith in freedom under the guidance of God. Freedom means the supremacy of human rights everywhere. Our support goes to those who struggle to gain those rights or keep them. Our strength is in our unity of purpose.

To that high concept there can be no end save victory.

Excerpted from *Congressional Record*, by Franklin D. Roosevelt, 77th Cong., 1st Sess., January 6, 1941.

Now Is the Chance to Beat Hitler

Although Congress passed Roosevelt's Lend-Lease program in March 1941, debate still raged over the growing U.S. commitment to the Allies. Some argued that no matter the cost, Hitler's war machine had to be stopped. Author and lecturer Stanley High was one who believed the United States should not hesitate to aid the Allied cause in any way possible. He even advocated that the time was ripe for full American commitment—including a formal declaration of war. On a May 1941 radio debate program called American Forum of the Air, *High reasoned that if Hitler could conquer all of Europe, he would soon turn on the United States for its past support of the Allies. Therefore, America should join the Allies now and ensure Germany's defeat.*

Either Hitler's defeat is of desperate, deadly importance to us or it's of no importance whatsoever. If his defeat is of desperate, deadly, importance then—now, immediately and at once—we have got to go all-out and whole-hog to defeat him. If his defeat is of no importance to us—then we've got to stop slapping his wrists, let him devour Britain and stock its bones in the New Order mausoleum where the remains of his other victims are lodged. It's one or the other. To say we want Hitler's defeat and to try a delicate side-step at the all-out job of defeating him is, first, a guarantee that he'll win; it's second, a guarantee that, having won, he'll hate us with a hatred

backed up by the resources of four-fifths of the world; and, third, it's a doctrine of turn-tail defeatism that's a travesty on everything American and an insult to the memory of those who—in blood and toil and tears and sweat—gave us America.

I think that Hitler's defeat is of desperate, deadly importance to us and that the time has come to stop aiming at his wrists and aim for his chin—and do it with the total armed might of the United States of America.

To do that may take us to war. Granted. But not to do it won't keep us at peace; not, that is, the kind of peace in which decency has elbowroom and the free spirit of man can go to work mending the torn fabric of our civilization. In this world there isn't any of that peace.

In this world there is peace of two sorts: There is the kind of peace that's come to the Poles, the Czechs, the Norwegians, and now the Greeks. If all you mean by peace is an absence of fighting—then those people have it. But if by peace you mean the defense and nurture of those inalienable rights among which are life, liberty and the pursuit of happiness—then the peace of those peoples is the peace of the dead.

There's another kind of peace we can have. We're getting it already. It's the peace of an armed camp—in which, for the indefinable future, our resources, our energies and our skills will be of use only as fuel for the engines of war and our lives of use only if they're bound and shackled to the war machine. That's the kind of peace the isolationists prescribe. That's why with almost one accord in Congress, they vote to load down our democracy with multiplied military billions and our nation with a wholly alien, completely militarized way of life. They're willing to do that because they know that, if we don't beat Hitler today, we've got to keep ready to beat him tomorrow—any tomorrow.

That kind of peace—for a grim interlude—may have no fighting in it. But neither will it have in it any room for those creative ventures, those civilized dreams and undertakings by which man, one day, may redeem himself from beastliness. That's the other kind of peace—the only other kind—we can have. It means a world—and a United States of America—whose moral climate will be fixed, not by the aspirations of free men, but by the blood-lusting ambitions of Adolf Hitler.

That becomes more sure with every Nazi victory. Today can be ours. Tomorrow certainly will be Hitler's. Today we've got Allies. Tomorrow we'll have none. Today, the British control the seas. Tomorrow they won't. Today Hitler has the continent of Europe. Tomorrow he and his associate plunderers will control four-fifths of the earth and its resources. Today our production can be decisive. Tomorrow in every warmaking asset Hitler will out-match us five, ten, twenty, to one. Today—there's hope and, therefore, resistance among the people he has conquered. Tomorrow, hope having died, these people will not only be conquered, they'll be subdued. Today his

ideological missionaries in South America are making headway against odds. Tomorrow—as emissaries of an unbeatable, world-conquering regime there'll be a wholesale flocking to their banners? Today Hitler's American kinsmen work under cover or wrapped in the flag. Tomorrow, they'll strut their foul stuff in the open.

Adolf Hitler surveys his troops at a 1933 Nazi rally. The strength of Hitler and his army worried many Americans.

With that Nazi noose round our necks, what chance will there be for that working democracy for which men like Norman Thomas [presidential candidate for the Socialist Party] so long have labored? Our social gains, our civil liberties and the dreams and ambitions of our younger generation will be swallowed up in the dire needs of a nation with its back to the wall. Give our youth five–ten years of that and at the end— the ways and the fruits of freedom will be as strange to them as they are to the youth of Germany.

The people of the United States aren't of a surrendering breed. They won't surrender now. They won't surrender—because what's at stake is more than a place on the map which we can call our own. What's at stake is the chance for us and for our children to call our lives our own. We can either beat Hitler now—or we can deliver into his hands the power to fashion our future.

Excerpted from Stanley High's remarks on *American Forum of the Air* radio broadcast, May 4, 1941.

Total War Risks the Spread of Fascism

On the May 4, 1941, American Forum of the Air *radio broadcast, Norman Thomas, a former Presbyterian minister and long-standing presidential candidate for the Socialist Party, spoke out against further U.S. commitment in the war. Thomas argued that it was hypocritical for America to stand back and ask other nations to fight against fascism when America, itself, was not willing to take part in that fight. Far from advocating that the United States take up that burden, Thomas insisted that U.S. involvement would only ensure a costly and prolonged war. He even hypothesized that the defeat of Hitler, if it could be achieved, would not necessarily bring about the end of fascism. Thomas suggested that Britain and America might become despotic imperial powers once the Axis nations are quieted and the built-up Allied armies have no cause left to fight.*

How far should the United States go to insure the defeat of Hitler? Well, after all, it isn't Hitler the man, but Hitlerism that is the disease, and there is a great deal too much emphasis on one mortal man, and Hitlerism isn't born of the devil; it is born of a bad system. I believe we should go not so far as to insure the triumphs of an American Hitlerism, and that would be the probable consequence of our entry into total war far more probably than under any other circumstances. The issue we are discussing in reality is war, total war, of indefinite duration which will have to be fought on the Atlantic, the Pacific, in Asia, Africa and Europe. To continue wishful and unrealistic thinking or desperate gambling on anything else but war is intellectual stupidity and moral hypocrisy. We cut a sorry figure telling other people that they must fight on and on unless we are willing to fight. Our present tactics are hurtful to our own morale and our reputation. I disagree with this new Fight for Freedom Committee but have a respect for it that I do not feel for these who believe we can take further steps short of war.

German soldiers in formation at a Nazi rally.

To be specific it is still as true as when the President stated the fact that convoys mean shooting and shooting almost certainly means war. Even if it doesn't, I do not suppose there are five advocates of convoys in all Washington who will not admit, if they are honest, that naval convoys alone cannot guarantee complete British victory. If that is our goal the cry for convoys will be just one more maneuver to get an unwilling people into war. Against dive bombers convoys don't mean much unless we send out fighter planes to protect them. Thus do we stumble towards war.

The question is, ought we to go to war? It is not a question to be answered simply by contemplating the undeniable crimes of the Nazi regime or by asserting what I have always admitted, namely that British Imperialism offers fewer dangers to America than German and is less of a curse to the earth.

The question is whether the means of full entry into this war by America will gain the end of peace and freedom for mankind or, to put it in another form, whether the dangers which our entry into war will bring upon us are not greater than any conceivable dangers which may come upon us if we stay out of war.

A wise Government policy must face probabilities. It must deal with them as scientifically as it can in the spirit of the engineer, the scientist or the surgeon who recognizes the limits to what can be done by wishful thinking and the impossibility of achieving the desirable simply because it is desirable.

The possibilities serious enough to deserve attention are these: (1) a German victory, before an America unprepared for aggressive long range war, can make her weight felt; (2) a complete Anglo-American victory over the Axis and probably Japan, after a long and costly struggle; (3) some degree of stalemate with exhaustion and then perhaps Stalin as the final victor. It is this third possibility which seems to me, on the evidence, the most probable. Any of these possibilities, given the realities of war, America's own unsolved problems, and the American temperament, will require us to lose our internal democracy for the dura-

tion of the war. The reaction to an unpopular and bitterly costly war will make for an indefinite continuance of conditions wholly unsuitable to democracy. On the other hand, victory would be accompanied, not by the achievement of the noble purposes which a minority of the interventionists profess, but by an American or Anglo-American imperialism which would perpetuate armaments, and for which Fascism at home in this generation must be the inevitable accompaniment. Against this there is a far better possibility of our blessing ourselves and ultimately mankind by making our own democracy work in the relative security of this continent, yes, and of a hemisphere which we can make friendly by the right sort of statesmanship. The real question is how far should the United States go to preserve and increase democracy rather than to spread Fascism by spreading the area of total war?

Excerpted from Narman Thomas's remarks on *American Forum of the Air* radio broadcast, May 4, 1941.

Letter to the Japanese Emperor

While the United States was supporting the Allied cause in Europe, it was also keenly aware of the aggressive actions of the Japanese Imperial Government in Southeast Asia. Japan had already been at war with China since 1931, and by late 1941, the Japanese had built up its forces and established military bases throughout the islands of Indochina. President Franklin D. Roo-

sevelt acknowledged the threat to the security of American possessions in the region. In a letter to the emperor of Japan, Roosevelt outlines the current situation and emphasizes how Japan's military posturing in the Pacific gives the impression that it is bent on conquest and not the peaceful defense of its borders.

Almost a century ago the President of the United States addressed to the Emperor of Japan a message extending an offer of friendship of the people of the United States to the people of Japan. That offer was accepted, and in the long period of unbroken peace and friendship which has followed, our respective nations, through the virtues of their peoples and the wisdom of their rulers have prospered and have substantially helped humanity.

Only in situations of extraordinary importance to our two countries need I address to Your Majesty messages on matters of state. I feel I should now so address you because of the deep and far-reaching emergency which appears to be in formation.

Developments are occurring in the Pacific area which threaten to deprive each of our nations and all humanity of the beneficial influence of the long peace between our two countries. Those developments contain tragic possibilities.

The people of the United States, believing in peace and in the right of nations to live and let live, have eagerly watched the conversations between our two Governments during these past months. We have hoped for a termination of the present conflict between Japan and China. We have hoped that a peace of the Pacific could be consummated in such a way that nationalities of many diverse peoples could exist side by side without fear of invasion; that unbearable burdens of armaments could be lifted for them all; and that all peoples would resume commerce without discrimination against or in favor of any nation.

I am certain that it will be clear to Your Majesty, as it is to me, that in seeking these great objectives both Japan and the United States should agree to eliminate any form of military threat. This seemed essential to the attainment of the high objectives. . . .

During the past few weeks it has become clear to the world that Japanese military, naval and air forces have been sent to

Japanese soldiers in China in 1935. By 1941, the Japanese had established a large military presence throughout Indochina.

Southern Indo-China in such large numbers as to create a reasonable doubt on the part of other nations that this continuing concentration in Indo-China is not defensive in its character.

Because these continuing concentrations in Indo-China have reached such large proportions and because they extend now to the southeast and the southwest corners of that Peninsula, it is only reasonable that the people of the Philippines, of the hundreds of Islands of the East Indies, of Malaya and of Thailand itself are asking themselves whether these forces of Japan are preparing or intending to make attack in one or more of these many directions.

I am sure that Your Majesty will understand that the fear of all these peoples is a legitimate fear inasmuch as it involves their peace and their national existence. I am sure that Your Majesty will understand why the people of the United States in such large numbers look askance at the establishment of military, naval and air bases manned and equipped so greatly as to constitute armed forces capable of measures of offense.

It is clear that a continuance of such a situation is unthinkable.

None of the peoples whom I have spoken of above can sit either indefinitely or permanently on a keg of dynamite.

There is absolutely no thought on the part of the United States of invading Indo-China if every Japanese soldier or sailor were to be withdrawn therefrom.

I think that we can obtain the same assurance from the Governments of the East Indies, the Governments of Malaya and the Government of Thailand. I would even undertake to ask for the same assurance on the part of the Government of China. Thus a withdrawal of the Japanese forces from Indo-China would result in the assurance of peace throughout the whole of the South Pacific area.

I address myself to Your Majesty at this moment in the fervent hope that Your Majesty may, as I am doing, give thought in this definite emergency a way of dispelling the dark clouds. I am confident that both of us, for the sake of the peoples not only of our own great countries but for the sake of humanity in neighboring territories, have a sacred duty to restore traditional amity and prevent further death and destruction in the world.

Excerpted from "Message to the Emperor of Japan," by Franklin D. Roosevelt, *Department of the State Bulletin*, December 13, 1941.

Eyewitness to Pearl Harbor

On Sunday morning, December 7, 1941, roughly 350 Japanese war planes from six aircraft carriers launched a surprise attack on the U.S. naval installation at Pearl Harbor, Hawaii. Their target was the American Pacific fleet, most of which was docked in the harbor. Within a short time, six of eight U.S. battleships were either sunk or heavily damaged. A handful of smaller ships were also seriously crippled by Japanese bombers, as were most of the American planes stationed at nearby airfields. Overall, twenty-four hundred Ameri-

cans were killed and another twelve hundred were wounded in the attack.

Lieutenant Commander Paul E. Spangler was a surgeon stationed with his family at Pearl Harbor. He witnessed the attack and wrote of it in a letter to his hunting buddies, the "Izee Reds," back in Portland, Oregon. Spangler notes how the Japanese seemed to know exactly when to strike, hinting that the Japanese were thoroughly informed of the navy's movements. Strangely, there had been many warning signs that an attack was imminent. Ambassador Joseph Grew had reported from Tokyo as early as January 1941 that Japan intended to bomb Pearl Harbor when tensions between the two nations peaked. Still, despite the warnings, the personnel at Pearl Harbor were taken completely by surprise. Luckily, the aircraft carriers of the U.S. Pacific fleet were out at sea on that fateful morning. With its carriers still in operation, America was not powerless, and Japanese naval strategists knew they had not achieved total victory.

Izee Reds:

Just a note to tell you hams that you ain't seen no shootin yet. We had a little disturbance out here a week ago Sunday and it was sumpin. I must hasten to tell you that we all survived it without a scratch but I expected to see my maker most any moment that Sunday morning. They are begining to evacuate those who want to go but the family will stay here untill ordered home.

I was resting peacefully in bed when I noticed rather more "practice fire" than I had heard before and then I realized that it

Fire and smoke fill the air over the naval air station at Pearl Harbor during the 1941 Japanese air attack.

was strange to be practicing on Sunday morning. About that time Clara and the kids came home from Church and their curiosity was aroused. Then I got the fatal word to report to the Hospital immediatley. I still was not certain what was going on untill I came off of the hill on my way to the Hospital. Then I saw the smoke from the several fires and saw the antiaircraft shells exploding. I opened her up then and with my Pearl Harbor plates on I had the right of way and I was out there in nothing flat. I arrived just in the lull between waves of attacks about 30 minutes after the first shooting.

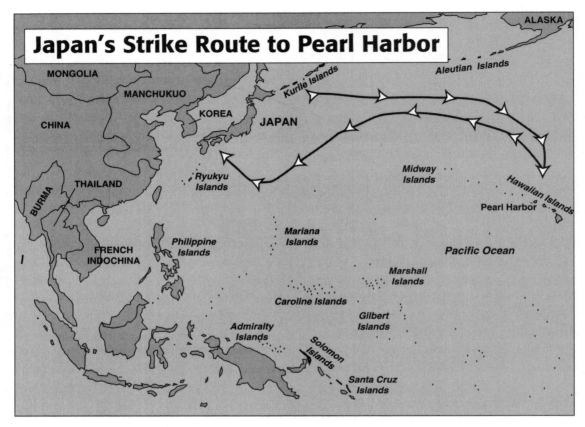

Japan's Strike Route to Pearl Harbor

There was one big Jap bomber in the sky flying over Hickam Field and Fort Kamahamaha but no one seemed to be doing anything about it. One Jap plane was down in flames at the Hospital and it had fired the Laboratory and one of the quarters which fortunatley had been vacated because they were starting a big new dry dock. I met the Exec. at the door and he told me to go up and take charge of the Surgery. . . .

I spent the next 72 hours in four hour shifts at the operating table. During my first shift we were under almost constant bombing and the A-A fire kept up a constant din.

They didn't actually hit the hospital but one explosion was so close it blew all the windows out of the work room which was right next to the room I was operating in. I thought my time had come for sure. It was hell for a while. These poor devils brought in all shot up and burned. Many of them hopeless. We gave them plenty of morphine and sent them out in the Wards to die. The others we patched up as best we could. . . .

You have read the official accounts given by the Secretary of the Navy. I note relief in the mainland that it was not as bad as feared. If the truth were known I don think they would be so optimistic. Dont quote me, but this is the real dope. We have just three battleships that can fight now. The Arizona and West Virginia are shambles. The Oklahoma is belly up and I doubt she will ever be of further use, if so it will be a full year. The California is sitting on the bottom but is still upright and may be salvaged. The Nevada is aground just across from the Hospital and they hope to float her this week but it will be a year before she can be fighting again. The Utah is a total wreck but she was not used except for training anyway. I think they thought she was a carrier as she was tied up at the carriers berth and they certainly gave her plenty. Four cruisers are badly damaged. Three destroyers are gone. Aircraft lost are certaily over two hundred. The hangers at Hickam Field, the mess hall, post exchange are all shot to hell. Many Flying Fortresses and PBYs [Scout planes] destroyed.

If you think these damn slant eyes didnt do a thorough job, guess again. They certainly knew where they could hurt us most and they droped their bombs and torpedos right there. They had all the information. They needed even to the exact location of the most vital targets and as to our ship movements and disposition. I cant understand why they soft pedal things back there. I think the people should know the truth. Then they would be roused to the necessary pitch to bring this thing to a successfull conclusion. It is not going to be an easy job in my opinion. I only hope the country will now take off their coats and go to work. We have the ability and skill but it is going to mean many sacrifices for all and a long

hard pull. What we need is planes, carriers, and subs. Thousands of them. . . .

I must close now and get this on its way. Please do not broadcast the source of this information as I am in a bad spot I guess if I was caught sending this sort of dope. But I thought you all would like to know the real dope and I think you should. . . .

We all send you our love and best wishes. We wish you all a Merry Christmas and A Happy New Year. And Remember Pearl Harbor.

Paul

A Date That Will Live in Infamy

The day after the Japanese raid on Pearl Harbor, President Franklin D. Roosevelt asked Congress for a formal declaration of war against Japan. In his speech before the legislature, Roosevelt cites the Japanese government's history of political deception as well as the aggressive attacks upon Hawaii and other U.S. possessions in the Pacific. Calling Japan's actions "unprovoked," the president demands the nation to turn its full might against such treachery.

Yesterday, December 7, 1941—a date which will live in infamy—the United States of America was suddenly and deliberately attacked by naval and air forces of the Empire of Japan.

The United States was at peace with that nation and, at the solicitation of Japan, was still in conversation with its government and its Emperor looking toward the maintenance of peace in the Pacific. Indeed, one hour after Japanese air squadrons had commenced bombing in Oahu, the Japanese ambassador to the United States and his colleague delivered to the Secretary of State [Cordell Hull] a formal reply to a recent American message. While this reply stated that it seemed useless to continue the existing diplomatic negotiations, it contained no threat or hint of war or armed attack.

It will be recorded that the distance of Hawaii from Japan makes it obvious that the attack was deliberately planned many days or even weeks ago. During the intervening time the Japanese Government has deliberately sought to deceive the United States by false statements and expressions of hope for continued peace.

The attack yesterday on the Hawaiian Islands has caused severe damage to American naval and military forces. Very many American lives have been lost. In addition American ships have been reported torpedoed on the high seas between San Francisco and Honolulu.

Yesterday the Japanese government also launched an attack against Malaya.

Last night Japanese forces attacked Hong Kong.

Last night Japanese forces attacked Guam.

Last night Japanese forces attacked the Philippine Islands.

Last night the Japanese attacked Wake Island.

This morning the Japanese attacked Midway Island.

Japan has, therefore, undertaken a surprise offensive extending throughout the Pacific area. The facts of yesterday speak for themselves. The people of the United States have already formed their opinions

President Franklin D. Roosevelt signs the war declaration against Japan on December 8, 1941.

and well understand the implications to the very life and safety of our nation.

As Commander-in-Chief of the Army and Navy, I have directed that all measures be taken for our defense.

Always will we remember the character of the onslaught against us.

No matter how long it may take us to overcome this premeditated invasion, the American people in their righteous might will win through to absolute victory.

I believe I interpret the will of the Congress and of the people when I assert that we will not only defend ourselves to the uttermost but will make very certain that this form of treachery shall never endanger us again.

Hostilities exist. There is no blinking at the fact that our people, our territory and our interests are in grave danger.

With confidence in our armed forces— with the unbounding determination of our people—we will gain the inevitable triumph —so help us God.

I ask that the Congress declare that since the unprovoked and dastardly attack by Japan on Sunday, December 7th, a state of war has existed between the United States and the Japanese Empire.

Excerpted from Franklin D. Roosevelt's war message delivered to the U.S. Congress, December 8, 1941.

Chapter 2

The Home Front

In the days following Japan's surprise attack on the U.S. fleet in Hawaii, the cry "Remember Pearl Harbor" served to unite the nation and give it a clear purpose. The future security of the United States, indeed the world, would depend on the defeat of the fascist aggressors. Almost overnight, the entire nation mobilized for war. Hundreds of thousands of young men volunteered for the military. Some women joined auxiliary military corps (support units that did not engage in fighting); others volunteered to serve as nurses in medical units that would be needed overseas. Still other women filled the factory jobs left vacant by the men who enlisted. Communities across the nation sponsored rubber and scrap metal drives to donate resources for wartime materials, or wrapped bandages for the Red Cross. The nation which had slumbered so long under the lean years of the Great Depression awoke to a bustling wartime economy.

While most Americans were called upon to support the war effort, there were segments of the population whose loyalty was questioned. German Americans, for example, endured taunts and accusations that their kinfolk in Europe were fighting for fascism. Japanese Americans fared even worse. They reminded many Americans of Pearl Harbor. Some government officials argued that the perfect surprise achieved at Pearl Harbor must have been in part due to the work of Japanese American spies working on the West Coast. To prevent further disasters, in February 1942 the Roosevelt administration issued Executive Order 9066, which ordered all Japanese Americans removed from western coastal states and sent to relocation camps in the deserts of Utah and Arizona. Around 112,000 men, women, and children were forced to make the journey to these barren prisons. They would remain in these camps—making the best of an unjust situation—until 1944. When eventually freed, many returned to their old neighborhoods only to find their jobs gone and their homes taken by new tenants. Supreme Court Justice Frank Murphy referred to the government's action as "one of the most sweeping and complete deprivations of constitutional rights in the history of this nation." Unfortunately, many of those detainees wanted only to support their new homeland in the war effort and considered abiding by the relocation order as their patriotic duty.

Another group of Americans eager to partake in the nation's struggle was the growing African American community. Nearly a million black Americans signed up with the armed forces over the course of the war and roughly half of them served overseas. Joining the military was not a problem for blacks, but fair treatment while in service was a challenge. America was still a nation divided by racial prejudice. Although the military was easing its previous restrictions on the types of service black men could perform and the ranks they could achieve, all branches of the service were still segregated during the war. African Americans were typically relegated to all black units, and many of these units were not given combat assignments. Despite this, black servicemen were

Actress Rita Hayworth (left) joined Americans across the country in donating car bumpers and used tires for the war effort.

PLEASE DRIVE CAREFULLY.
MY BUMPERS ARE ON THE SCRAP HEAP

proud of their accomplishments. The few who did see combat—especially in the European theater—earned distinction and were praised by their white commanders. Their bravery and achievements helped change military policy, although the armed services would not be desegregated until well after the war.

The United States weathered the Second World War quite well. Other than the raid on Pearl Harbor, the nation was never directly threatened by attack. Its isolation from the battlefields of Europe and Asia allowed America to become what President Roosevelt termed "the great arsenal of democracy." Industrial production increased significantly, and America was able to build its own military while still supplementing those of England, France, and Russia. As the nation turned all its efforts to defeat the world's dictators, the hardships and sluggish economy of the depression years were all but forgotten. Although rationing of food and other war materials was the norm during the war, the rejuvenation of the economy and the spirit of nationalism helped make the nation prosperous in the coming decades.

Signing Up

After the Japanese bombed Pearl Harbor, a patriotic fever swept America. Young men from all walks of life flooded military enlistment posts. Most were given routine exams, and even if the enlistee failed, many recruiters were willing to *look the other way to increase the pool of eligible servicemen. Not all young men volunteered, however. Many had deferments that let them remain civilians for years. Others were called into service through the Selective Service law (the draft) that was first established in 1940. By 1943, the U.S. Army, alone, would have over 8 million personnel. The influx of men boosted the sagging Allied war effort and helped turn the tide of the war.*

HARRY BARE: "I was born and raised in Philadelphia, Pennsylvania, in 1914. [By] 1942, Pearl Harbor had been bombed, and we were in it. I was young, in good shape, and they were not going to have a war without me. We did not have ROTC at my college, but I did learn about VOC, Volunteer's Officer Candidate School, and thought, that's for me. I signed up, and at Fort Niagara took all the tests and qualified in all except the physical. After three days, I was washed out for high blood pressure.

"Disappointed and angry, I went right down and enlisted. Strange, but I passed my physical with flying colors. Not a word was said about high blood pressure. I was assigned to the 269th Ordnance Service Battalion as a T-5 but realized that this was not for me, so I joined the 116th Infantry Regiment, 29th Division, 2nd Battalion, F Company, as a buck sergeant. I received another stripe, and as a staff sergeant was in charge of 1st Squad, F Company."

ROBERT HEALEY: "I was born in Somerville, Massachusetts, on May 7, 1919. I was first called up in February of 1942. I was turned down for poor eyesight and was very disappointed, because like everyone else of that day, people of my age wanted to be in the service because all of our friends were there. I was hoping for another chance, and that chance came in November of 1942 when I was again called up and sent for a physical. Luckily for me, the army used an eye chart with a large *E* and with progressively smaller letters as you went down. Standing in line with my glasses on, I memorized the whole chart, so when it came time to take the test, I passed. A clerk who was there remarked to the doctor that on my previous test my eyes had been much worse, and the doctor told the clerk, 'Mind your own business. Go ahead, kid.' I was in, and I was tickled.

"The command I was sent to was the 149th Combat Engineers; I was assigned to A Company, 1st Platoon."

MARTIN FRED GUTEKUNST (Signalman 3rd Class, U.S. Navy): "I had a high draft number, so I thought the conflict would be over before I was drafted. By 1943, after a series of defense industry deferments, and with a constant reminder from mothers who had sons in the army saying to me, 'How come you're still around here?—my son has been in for so many years,' I was anxious to join them.

"At the induction center, I was asked which branch of service I preferred. My choice was the Air Corps. However, the authorities in charge directed me to a table with a lot of uniformed men. They said, 'You are now in the navy.'

"We did some dry landings and were taught how to dig foxholes. We soon began to realize that we were not in the navy as we had known the navy to be. This was the amphibious, which was new, and somewhat disorganized. Somewhere our unit was named JASCAL, or Joint Assault Signal Company."

FRED PATHEIGER: "I was born on December 22, 1919, in Rastatt, Germany. When I was a year old, my mother and father were divorced. I lived with my mother, grandmother, and aunt. When Hitler got into power, my mother, grandmother, and aunt had to join the [Nazi] party. I had to join the Hitler Youth or I couldn't have gone to school, and I discovered one day while a youngster crawling into the living room and listening to these ladies speak that much to my amazement, my grandfather on my mother's side was Jewish.

"My aunt went with a fellow. They were going to get married and she told him about her background, and when he found out that her father had been Jewish, well, that was it. He reported it and we were all in trouble. We had to get out of the party; I had to get out of the Hitler Youth. This was in the mid-thirties, and of course, I continued to go to school, and my mother made overtures to distant relatives in Chicago to get me out of the country. I would have been nothing but cannon fodder.

"A distant cousin put up an affidavit, and I came over here in April, 1938. The others remained over there. We tried to get them over here, but the Nazis kept bringing up one obstacle after another. We finally had everything set and had made arrangements to bring them over via Japan, but then Pearl Harbor happened, and that did not work out. Eventually, they succumbed in the concentration camps.

"I got into the service in December, 1942. I volunteered for the Air Corps—glider. I was the typical ninety-pound weakling pictured in Charles Atlas ads until paratrooper training. That completely changed me. I was now one of the elite; I was a Screaming Eagle of the 101st Airborne Division."

Excerpted from *Voices of D-Day: The Story of the Allied Invasion Told by Those Who Were There*, edited by Ronald J. Drez (Baton Rouge, LA, Louisiana State University Press, 1996). Copyright © 1996 by Louisiana State University Press. Reprinted with permission.

Since You Went Away

While military personnel were off fighting in Europe and the Pacific, friends and families went on with their lives in the United States. Although people on the home front endured rubber shortages, gas shortages, and even food shortages, they knew their predicament was not as tough as the young men risking their lives overseas. Wives, sweethearts, parents, siblings, and friends kept in touch with the soldiers through numerous letters. They often discussed daily life as well as news of the war. The servicemen looked forward to mail call just to take comfort in the normalcy of home life.

Catherine "Renee" Pike was one of many wives who kept up regular correspondence with a husband overseas. George Pike was drafted into the army in 1942, while Renee was pregnant with their first child, Little Georgie. Writing from their home in Esmond, Rhode Island, Renee kept George updated on life in the small town.

Esmond, Feb. 3, 1943
My darling Husband,

Last night I had a whole mix-up of dreams. But one thing I dreamed was that I was eating banana splits one right after the other and were they good! When I awakened I thought to myself "Boy, what I wouldn't give for a nice banana." But that is just wishful thinking. I don't think anyone in America has seen a banana for over six months.

Well, George, the civilian population is certainly feeling the shortage of food-stuffs now. Last week we didn't have a scratch of butter in the house from Monday until Friday—and how I hate dry bread! It's a lot worse on we people in the country than it is on the city folks. They can go out and get some kind of meat every day while we have plenty of meatless days up here. They can also stand in line for 2 or 3 hours for a pound of butter, but up here there are no lines as there is no butter and when there is a little butter everyone gets a ¼ of a pound. So you can imagine how far a ¼ of a pound goes in this family of five adults. And that's suppose to last us for a week.

Yesterday I didn't take any meat not because we didn't have any but because I'm sick of the same thing. You see, the thing that they have the most of is sausages, but people can't keep eating the same thing every day. . . .

I received a swell letter from you yesterday. Gee, it seems that all the letters I've got from you recently have been the nicest letters. . . . I love you, George, more than anything in the whole, wide world.

Yours forever, Renee

Esmond, March 4, 1943
My Darling.

I've just been thinking that you'll miss getting my letters when I go to the hospital, won't you? . . .

I'm beginning to get weary now and nervous. I want to go and get it over with. You see, Darling, I've gained 25 pounds since I first started [the pregnancy] and at the end like this you get sort of miserable. Last night after I got to bed I had what is known as "false labor." I had quite bad pains in my stomach but I didn't tell anyone and I dropped off to sleep after awhile. But it makes you think that your time has come, believe me. . . .

Honey, whether I've had the baby or whether I haven't why don't you ask for a furlough when you're through with your schooling. Of course you know better than me if you should but let me know what you think about it. O.K.?

I want to see you so much, Honey, and I miss you something awful, especially lately. I love you with all my heart and soul and body.

Yours forever, Renee

Excerpted from *Since You Went Away: World War II Letters from American Women on the Home Front,* edited by Judy Barrett Litoff and David C. Smith (New York: Oxford University Press, 1991).

We Just Enjoyed Ourselves Completely

Although the war brought hardships to many people on the home front, some aspects of life did not change. Emily Koplin was in high school in Milwaukee, Wisconsin, during the early war years, and upon graduation in 1943 she joined the Allen-Bradley Company. In an interview fifty years later, Emily recalls rationing and other privations, but she fondly recounts the fun she and her girlfriends had while waiting for the young men to return from the war.

What were some of the first changes that you can recall occurring in your life as a result of the war?

The rationing. I think the part that hurt us the most was the gas rationing and the tightness of food—meat. I remember my mother going to grocery stores and coming home with just a small package of whatever. There was no variety, [and] whatever they had, she bought.

What was dating like during the war?

The girls that I knew all had boyfriends who were in the service and we didn't date because we were "tagged." I was going out with a fellow that was in the air force and I had his wings and he also sent me his lieutenant wings. . . . I spent a lot of time with the girls that I worked with [at Allen-Bradley] who had boyfriends or husbands overseas. There wasn't much dating going on. Most of the girls had engagement rings and we were all busy writing letters and corresponding, so the dating was mostly girls with girls. I don't know about the others, but that's the crowd that I went with. We waited for our men to come home. We didn't do any dating—those were the years where we would go to dances and girls would dance with girls. We had good times; we had a lot of fun. We were very, very close because we were all waiting for [our men] to come back home. We had a lot in common and were very close.

What sorts of things would you do when you would go out with your girlfriends?

We went to a lot of movies. . . . We did a lot of dancing, and we spent a lot of time—we used to spend days down at the parks and down at the lakefront posing for pic-

People wait in line to buy rations of sugar. The U.S. government rationed many products during the war years.

tures. It sounds so silly now, but we used to spend days posing for pictures and sunbathing so that it would look good in the pictures.

Even though there was rationing, we used to go out a lot. I remember never going home after work. We used to always go someplace and eat and then the girls would get together at somebody's house. We played ping-pong, we played cards, we bowled, we did a lot of just really nothing. We kept busy. We used to have ping-pong tournaments to see who the champion was, and we really worked at it. We spent whole nights beating each other to see who the winner was. We just enjoyed ourselves completely. We used to go to baseball games. And, of course, once I joined Allen-Bradley, Allen-Bradley held baseball games. The company belonged to an industrial league. We also had basketball games right here in the shop. We used to go up to the gym in evenings and I was part of the Allen-Bradley Dramatic Club. We used to put on shows here and we'd have to rehearse nights. So, we kept busy, very busy.

Do you think there was a special sense of camaraderie among women during the war?

Yes, very definitely.

What did that mean to you in terms of creating friendships among women?

My family—I had a mother and a father and a brother. When I started working here at Allen-Bradley, and of course those were the war years, all the girls—we were very, very close. It was like we were all sisters. There was a closeness that you don't have

today. A lot of the girls that were working here were from out of town, didn't have families in Milwaukee. . . . We were much closer than the women are today, much closer. And we all cried on each other's shoulders and we knew everything about everybody. We knew when they got letters from their boyfriends, we knew when they didn't feel good, we knew when they were going home to, let's say, Pulaski, Wisconsin. We knew just exactly where we all were almost on an hourly basis. It was a very close knit—the women were stuck together much more than today. . . .

It was very important to have somebody to lean on, to have somebody to just talk to. Here's a situation where even though I was at home with my mother and my father, I couldn't relate to them like I related to these other gals because we all had the same feelings about what was happening. And the mothers and the fathers, they were worried about their sons being overseas, not necessarily the daughter that was left back home. They were concentrating on bringing their boys back home. So I think that that's one of the reasons why the girls—that we did become as friendly as we did with one another.

Was the war the crucial element in bringing women together?

Yes, I believe so. Because we all had so much in common and leaned on one another. I don't think that would have happened if the girls would have been married to these gentlemen and would have started their families. Then they would have had their separate lives and gone [their separate ways], because that's what happened when the war ended. That's what happened with the war. As these men came home and the girls married and they started having their families then all of a sudden those of us who weren't married or didn't get married, then you're not part of that pattern anymore. They would go their way and you would go your way. The ending of the war made everybody go in "their own directions."

Excerpted from *Women Remember the War: 1941–1945*, edited by Michael E. Stevens (Madison, WI: State Historical Society, 1993). Copyright © 1993 by State Historical Society of Wisconsin. Reprinted with permission.

Joining the WAAC

During World War II women were not allowed to enlist in combat commands in the armed services, but they were allowed to join the military in auxiliary outfits. The Women's Army Auxiliary Corps (WAAC), for example, took in thousands of volunteers. Frieda Schurch was a Wisconsin native who signed up with the WAAC in 1943. In this interview from the 1990s, Schurch reflects on what it was like to join the WAAC and how the women's corps differed from the regular army at the time. Schurch was posted to Iowa, Texas, and eventually a base in Florida where she would first encounter German soldiers—prisoners of war sent to military camps to do cooking and other menial labor. She stayed in the WAAC until her discharge in 1945, around the time when the organization was making the transition to the abbreviated Women's Army Corps (WAC).

What prompted you to join the WAACs?

I decided that there was just no future on the farm as a housekeeper and I wasn't being accepted as a partner because the farmers were the partners, [and] I was the housekeeper. When I read about the WAACs, [it] fascinated me.

How did you find out about the WAACs?

We always had a newspaper and often got another Sunday paper. It was always stressed [that] we had to read what was going on; we had to know what was going on in the world and the community. My folks were adults when they came to this country, but they wanted us always to know what was going on. And so of course there were articles on the WAACs in those newspapers, and I decided that was a great thing for me and was a good way of getting out, because I really didn't know when I was ever going to get back to college. I came home to take care of my mother and my mother had died, but now that evolved into being the housekeeper and now I wanted to see an end, going back to school, but I didn't see it. . . . So I simply drove the car to Barneveld and saw a doctor, who had to sign that I was in good health, and then I sent the papers in. . . .

How did the army treat the WAACs?

Drew Field [in Tampa] was run by regular army people, and regular army people did not want women on the base, . . . so they put us five miles out, of the base, in a swamp area that wasn't drained and had mosquitoes. They had built four barracks and a mess hall. And then we had a bus that came every morning and came every night and you better get out there at five, and you were supposed to work until five so you had to run. Every night at five it rained and so you ran through the rain and got in the bus and went to the barracks. . . .

We were not a hundred WAACs at the base, but we always averaged fourteen in the hospital for infected mosquito bites. And I came home once during that time, and my legs react to mosquito bites, but otherwise mosquitoes can land on my arm and I don't react. In those days it took forty-four hours on the train to get from Tampa Field to Barneveld, . . . and if I sit up that long then my legs swell, and between the swelling of my legs and all those mosquito bites, my dad looked at my legs and said, "Is that what you went in the service for?" He said, "You'd never have those kind of legs at home, and you wouldn't have them now."

But, anyway, we were then discharged [during the transition from the WAAC to WAC], and there were two women who were a little older, had been around a little more than me, that's for sure, and were from the New York City area and they had a little money and they simply got out of the service. . . . [They] took a place on the beach at St. Petersburg, which was near Tampa, and then they could write directly to Washington, D.C. You didn't have to go through any chain anymore, and [they] told them what conditions we were living under in Tampa, Florida, Drew Field, and then we were moved out of there. . . . Then

A WAAC publicity poster. The WAAC provided women with work opportunities unavailable during peacetime.

later, as time went on, [the army] decided that area was built up and they could use that for the German war prisoners, but it did not pass the Geneva Accord and so it had to be drained, because of the mosquitoes. But we lived under [those conditions]. See, we were not part of the army then, we were WAAC, and the old army was in charge of the base, and they always made rulings that exempted the women [from equal treatment].

Did you expect this sort of treatment when you joined the military?

I didn't think it was right, but it wasn't so over-shocking and you just kept fighting it. . . . The officer of the headquarters called all the WAACs who worked at headquarters back from seven to ten [in the evening], Monday, Wednesday, and Friday to work, but [he] had everything locked up so there was no work. And because

then you're more apt to break, if there's nothing to do. If they had come back, he figured, every night, and there was really emergency things to do, we would never break. But he had hopes that by calling those women back Monday, Wednesday, and Friday and having nothing to do from

A female mechanic works on a military airplane, a skill she learned in the WAAC.

seven to ten [when] they had to be there . . . that they would break. But they didn't.

What do you mean by "break"?

I mean a breakdown, a mental breakdown, a nervous breakdown [is] what it was called then. Yes, that's what they thought they could do. Then they'd be discharged for Section 8, which was not a good discharge, especially not then. . . .

After the POWs came, [to prevent fraternization,] we closed our mess hall because the German prisoners did the KP [Kitchen duties], . . . and we all ate with the men. And this one day this woman was in the line and as she went ahead, the man ahead of her stepped back, which can happen because he passed something and decided he wanted it. It was nothing mean, but they collided, and so her tray flew to the floor and there was a German war prisoner standing there with a mop and he came right over to clean up and he picked up the tray and handed it to her and she said, "Thank you," and the mess sergeant wanted her court-martialed for talking to a German war prisoner. And that went on for a while before it was thrown out. And our commanding officer said that every week she got a call, and the rumors and the stories got worse, [like] she was pregnant from the German war prisoner, to that extent, and therefore she needed to be court-martialed. And all that had happened actually was when she was handed that tray she said, "Thank you."

Excerpted from *Women Remember the War: 1941–1945*, edited by Michael E. Stevens (Madison, WI: State Historical Society, 1993). Copyright © 1993 by State Historical Society of Wisconsin. Reprinted with permission.

Japanese Americans Pose a National Security Risk

After the surprise attack on Pearl Harbor, a cautious and suspicious U.S. government was quick to implement measures to secure itself against spying and sabotage. Japanese Americans were the obvious target of these measures, because they were both a visible minority and a great number of them lived on the West Coast near America's Pacific naval stations and shore defenses. Several Japanese were immediately rounded up and detained, while others had their bank accounts and assets frozen.

Many Americans believed these precautions did not go far enough. Some columnists, radio commentators, and local officials called for the deportation of all Japanese residents. Earl Warren, the attorney general of California at the time, was one of the vocal proponents of deporting suspect "aliens." In 1942 he argued before a congressional committee that Japanese Americans posed a dangerous threat to the nation's security. Ironically, Warren would go on to become a chief justice of the Supreme Court from 1953 to 1969, during which time he became celebrated as a defender of civil liberties.

For some time I have been of the opinion that the solution of our alien enemy problem with all its ramifications, which include the descendants of aliens, is not only a Federal problem but is a military problem. We believe that all of the decisions in that regard must be made by the military command that is charged with the security of

I believe that up to the present and perhaps for a long time to come the greatest danger to continental United States is that from well organized sabotage and fifth-column activity.

California presents, perhaps, the most likely objective in the Nation for such activities. There are many reasons why that is true. First, the size and number of our naval and military establishments in California would make it attractive to our enemies as a field of sabotage. Our geographical position with relation to our enemy and to the war in the Pacific is also a tremendous factor. The number and the diversification of our war industries is extremely vital. The fire hazards due to our climate, our forest areas, and the type of building construction make us very susceptible to fire sabotage. Then the tremendous number of aliens that we have resident here makes it almost an impossible problem from the standpoint of law enforcement.

A wave of organized sabotage in California accompanied by an actual air raid or even by a prolonged black-out could not only be more destructive to life and property but could result in retarding the entire war effort of this Nation far more than the treacherous bombing of Pearl Harbor.

I hesitate to think what the result would be of the destruction of any of our big airplane factories in this State. It will interest you to know that some of our airplane factories in this State are entirely surrounded by Japanese land ownership or occupancy. It is a situation that is fraught with the great-

A Japanese American child waits to be evacuated to a detention center.

this area. I am convinced that the fifth-column activities [spying and sabotage] of our enemy call for the participation of people who are in fact American citizens, and that if we are to deal realistically with the problem we must realize that we will be obliged in time of stress to deal with subversive elements of our own citizenry. . . .

est danger and under no circumstances should it ever be permitted to exist. . . .

Unfortunately, however, many of our people and some of our authorities and, I am afraid, many of our people in other parts of the country are of the opinion that because we have had no sabotage and no fifth-column activities in this State since the beginning of the war, that means that none have been planned for us. . . .

And when I say "this State" I mean all of the coast, of course I believe that Oregon and Washington are entitled to the same sort of consideration as the zone of danger as California. Perhaps our danger is intensified by the number of our industries and the number of our aliens, but it is much the same. . . .

I want to say that the consensus of opinion among the law-enforcement officers of this State is that there is more potential danger among the group of Japanese who are born in this country than from the alien Japanese who were born in Japan. That might seem an anomaly to some people, but the fact is that, in the first place, there are twice as many of them. There are 33,000 aliens and there are 66,000 born in this country.

In the second place, most of the Japanese who were born in Japan are over 55 years of age. There has been practically no migration to this country since 1924. But in some instances the children of those people have been sent to Japan for their education, either in whole or in part, and while they are over there they are indoctrinated

with the idea of Japanese imperialism. They receive their religious instruction which ties up their religion with their Emperor, and they come back here imbued with the ideas and the policies of Imperial Japan.

While I do not cast a reflection on every Japanese who is born in this country—of course we will have loyal ones—I do say that the consensus of opinion is that taking the groups by and large there is more potential danger to this State from the group that is born here than from the group that is born in Japan. . . .

We believe that when we are dealing with the Caucasian race we have methods that will test the loyalty of them, and we believe that we can, in dealing with the Germans and the Italians, arrive at some fairly sound conclusions because of our knowledge of the way they live in the community and have lived for many years. But when we deal with the Japanese we are in an entirely different field and we cannot form any opinion that we believe to be sound. Their method of living, their language, make for this difficulty. Many of them who show you a birth certificate stating that they were born in this State, perhaps, or born in Honolulu, can hardly speak the English language because, although they were born here, when they were 4 or 5 years of age they were sent over to Japan to be educated and they stayed over there through their adolescent period at least, and then they came back here thoroughly Japanese. . . .

I had together about 10 days ago about 40 district attorneys and about 40 sheriffs in the State to discuss this alien problem. I asked all of them collectively at that time if in their experience any Japanese, whether California-born or Japan-born, had ever given them any information on subversive activities or any disloyalty to this country. The answer was unanimously that no such information had ever been given to them.

Now, that is almost unbelievable. You see, when we deal with the German aliens, when we deal with the Italian aliens, we have many informants who are most anxious to help the local authorities and the State and Federal authorities to solve this alien problem. They come in voluntarily and give us information. We get none from the other source. . . .

There is one thing that concerns us at the present time. As I say, we are very happy over the order of the President yesterday [Executive Order 9066]. We believe that is the thing that should be done, but that is only one-half of the problem, as we see it. It is one thing to take these people out of the area and it is another thing to do something with them after they get out. Even from the small areas that they have left up to the present time there are many, many Japanese who are now roaming around the State and roaming around the Western States in a condition that will unquestionably bring about race riots and prejudice and hysteria and excesses of all kind.

I hate to say it, but we have had some evidence of it in our State in just the last 2 or 3 days. People do not want these Japanese just loaded from one community to an-

other, and as a practical matter it might be a very bad thing to do because we might just be transposing the danger from one place to another.

So it seems to me that the next thing the Government has to do is to find a way of handling these aliens who are removed from any vital zone.

Excerpted from Earl Warren's statement before the House Select Committee Investigating Nation Defense Migration, 77th Cong., 2nd Sess., Feburary 21 & 23, 1942.

We Want to Be Treated as Americans

In early 1942 President Roosevelt issued Executive Order 9066, a plan to remove Japanese Americans from their homes near important military bases and other sensitive areas on the West Coast. Shortly after, a congressional committee was formed in the House of Representatives to examine the merits and legality of the order. In late February 1942, this committee (commonly referred to as the Tolan Committee after its chairman, Democratic representative John H. Tolan of California) held public hearings in California, Washington, and Oregon. Several local politicians like Earl Warren of California spoke in favor of forced evacuation in the name of public safety and national security. A few Japanese Americans, however, were allowed to testify against this extreme measure.

Michio Kunitani was one of fifteen Japanese Americans to speak at the hearings. Kunitani was a second generation Japanese American who had previously renounced his Japanese citizen-

ship and joined the Nisei Democratic Club of Oakland, an organization of second generation Japanese Americans who advocated education and political activism. Though he did not argue against mass evacuation per se, Kunitani denied the implied charges that Japanese Americans were disloyal to their adopted nation. In his testimony, he tries to explain away the fears other Americans may have of the Japanese immigrants. He also portrays Japanese Americans as patriotic citizens who want only to aid in the defense of their country.

We come here as Americans prepared to take a frank attitude and make frank statements, and speak to the members of this committee here just as people probably would in the cloakroom of the House of Representatives. . . .

We come here as Americans, not by virtue of our birth in America, but by virtue of the social and cultural forces in America. We come here to be treated as Americans and we want to live as Americans in America.

As I say, we are Americans, not by the mere technicality of birth, but by all the other forces of sports, amusements, schools, churches, which are in our communities and which affect our lives directly.

Some of us are Yankee fans; some of us are Dodger fans; some like to sip beer; some like to go up to the Top of the Mark once in a while; we enjoy Jack Benny; we listen to Beethoven, and some of us even go through the Congressional Record. That is something.

The main idea that our group wanted to present here today was that we didn't want to be treated as a special group of enemy aliens and as descendants of enemy aliens. We want to be treated as Americans, or as other groups, such as Italians, Yugoslavs, or Finns.

It seems that among the reasons put forth by the committee, and the witnesses who testified this morning, and last Saturday, on why they thought that we should be treated as a special group were the following:

No. 1. Our physical characteristics.

No. 2. The question of dual citizenship.

No. 3. The vague question of Shintoism and national religion.

The day after the attack on Pearl Harbor, this store's Japanese owner put up a sign declaring his loyalty to America.

No. 4. The question of the [Japanese] language schools which many of us have attended. . . .

I would like to touch on the question of loyalty. There has been a hue and cry by a lot of the people in California that there has been no anti-Fascist action on the part of any Japanese group. I would like to refute that statement right here and now.

Our organization, since the Democratic campaign of 1938, has come out on numerous occasions against shipments of oil and scrap iron to the Fascist war lords of Japan, and we opposed [Italy's] aggression in Ethiopia. Our records are filled with communications to our Congressmen, even to our Representative, who happens to be Mr. Tolan, urging them to vote against such measures in Congress. . . .

Now, I want to touch on the question of dual citizenship. I do not know very much about its history and background, but I can present my case in point.

I didn't even know that I was a citizen of Japan until I was about 17 years old, and a freshman in college. My father happened to tell me that I was a citizen of Japan. Therefore, I went through the legal channels and expatriated myself. . . .

Another thing I would like to point out to the members of the committee is the indivisibility of citizenship in the eyes of American law. If we are citizens here that is enough. I don't think all this cry about the question of dual citizenship is that important. I mean it doesn't play a major role in our lives. . . .

Another thing I would like to point out is this: Which came first, the defense areas or the Japanese farms that are around the defense areas?

I would like to point out that agriculture was the first occupation open to the Japanese people. The people who came here first were agriculturalists. One-third of the present Japanese population in the United States is engaged in agricultural pursuits. It just happens that they have followed a pattern. It is a similar pattern in Des Moines, Iowa, in Jamestown, Va. as well as in California. It is a social pattern which is not peculiar to California, or to Washington. The fundamental basis is the same all over the United States. . . .

Another point I want to bring out is about Pearl Harbor. We hear lots about sabotage at Pearl Harbor. . . . I can only go on the Roberts report, which was the only official United States document put out, as to what happened at Pearl Harbor, and why things happened as they did. I think if you gentlemen look into the Roberts report again you will find that no mention was made of sabotage on the part of Japanese-Americans. . . .

I mean to say the average Japanese in California isn't intelligent enough to go about and engage in fifth column activities. The odds are against him. He has an oriental face that can be easily detected.

I am not saying there wasn't any fifth column activity in Pearl Harbor on the part of Japanese, but I don't think there was wholesale fifth column activity on the part of the Japanese-Americans or the aliens in Pearl Harbor.

Excerpted from Michio Kunitani's statement before the House Select Committee Investigating Nation Defense Migration, 77th Cong., 2nd Sess., Feburary 21 & 23, 1942.

Relocation

Despite some protest, the U.S. Army carried out its orders to remove Japanese Americans from their homes on the West Coast and transport them to *detention camps in desert regions of California, Arizona, Utah, and other isolated places. Most Japanese Americans submitted without struggle, taking what possessions they could and locking up their homes. They endured the long bus and truck rides with stoicism, and moved in to the hastily constructed apartments at the camps. Although their new homes were bordered by barbed*

Japanese Americans eat in a mess hall at one of the many internment camps created during the war.

wire fences and guard towers, the Japanese Americans eventually established a community at the camps, resurrecting Boy Scout troops and other clubs that they had left behind.

Mary Tsukamoto was a California resident when the presidential order was put into effect. As a member of the Japanese American Citizens League (JACL), Tsukamoto helped others in her community comply with the relocation order. In this interview conducted in the 1980s, she describes the rampant confusion, the fear of FBI raids, and the pain of leaving behind all the Japanese American community had worked to achieve.

We tried to get everybody instructions, and the WCCA [Wartime Civilian Control Administration] would tell me one thing one day, and I would then tell everybody this is what we're going to need to do, and then the next week the whole regulation was changed, and we just ended up being liars right and left. It was such a state of confusion and anger, everyone being so upset at what was happening. I remember I was crying inside and I just felt like I was put through a hamburger machine. I was human and worried and scared for myself too, but worried about everybody else and trying to help people.

I remember Ida Onga. Her husband was taken by the FBI, and she came in here so big; she was going to have a baby in a month or so. She cried because she was supposed to go and see the doctor, and she didn't know that she had to have a traveler's permit. . . .

I remember Mrs. Kuima, whose son was thirty-two years old and retarded. She took

care of him. They had five other boys, but she took care of this boy at home. The welfare office said No, she couldn't take him, that the families have to institutionalize a child like that. It was a very tragic thing for me to have to tell her, and I remember going out to the field—she was hoeing strawberries—and I told her what they told us, that you can't take your son with you. And so she cried, and I cried with her.

I had anxieties for Grandpa and Grandma. They were old and had farmed all their lives, and after more than fifty years here, the thought of uprooting these people and taking them away from their farm and the things they loved was terrible. Grandpa growing tea and vegetables, and Grandma growing her flowers. It was a cruel thing to do to them in their twilight years. But we had to get them ready to leave, anxious for their health and their safety. And my daughter, who was five, had to be ready to go to school. Al [the author's husband] had had a hemorrhage that winter, so we all had our personal grief as well. . . .

We left early in the morning on May 29, 1942. Two days earlier we sold our car for eight hundred dollars, which was just about giving it away. We also had to sell our refrigerator. But some wonderful friends came to ask if they could take care of some things we couldn't store. Mr. Lernard, a principal of a high school, took my piano, and his daughter took our dining table set, which was a wedding gift. They did that for us. Other things we had to sell, and still other things we had to crate. . . .

It happened so suddenly to our community. You know, we grew up together, we went through the hardships of the Depression, and then finally things were picking up. People who had mortgages on their land were beginning to be able to make payments back to the bank. They were going to own the land that they had worked so hard to have. Then we had to evacuate. So there were still some people who owed some money on their property, and they lost the property because, of course, they couldn't make mortgage payments.

These were our people, and we loved them. We wept with them at their funerals and laughed with them and rejoiced at their weddings. And suddenly we found out that the community was going to be split up. The railroad track was one dividing line, and Florin Road the other dividing line. We were going to Fresno; the ones on the other side went to Manzanar; and the ones on the west side went to Tule. The ones on the west and north went to Pinedale and Poston. We never dreamed we would be separated—relatives and close friends, a community. The village people, we were just like brothers and sisters. We endured so much together and never dreamed we would be separated. Suddenly we found out we wouldn't be going to the same place. That was a traumatic disappointment and a great sadness for us. . . .

Early in the morning, Margaret and George File came after us in their car because we no longer had one to move our things. . . . It was such a clear, beautiful day, and I remember as we were driving, our tears. We saw the snow-clad Sierra Nevada mountains that we had loved to see so often, and I thought about God and about the prayer that we often prayed.

I remember one scene very clearly: on the train, we were told not to look out the window, but people were peeking out. After a long time on the train somebody said, "Oh, there's some Japanese standing over there." So we all took a peek, and we saw this dust, and rows and rows of barracks, and all these tan, brown Japanese people with their hair all bleached. They were all standing in a huddle looking at us, looking at this train going by. Then somebody on the train said, "Gee, that must be Japanese people in a camp." We didn't realize who they were before, but I saw how terrible it looked: the dust, no trees—just barracks and a bunch of people standing against the fence, looking out. Some children were hanging onto the fence like animals, and that was my first sight of the assembly center. I was so sad and discouraged looking at that, knowing that, before long, we would be inside too.

Excerpted from "Jerome," by Mary Tsukamoto, *Justice for All: An Oral History of the Japanese American Detention Camps*, edited by Jofn Tateishi (Seattle, WA: University of Washington Press, 1984). Copyright © 1984 by John Tateishi. Reprinted by permission of the University of Washington Press.

To Train at Tuskegee

Most American combat units in World War II were made up of white soldiers. Black Americans were typically relegated to supply service and other behind-the-lines duties. Late in the war, however, a few black combat units were formed and did serve with distinction in Germany. But on the home front, African Americans enlisted with the hopes that they, too, could help fight for their nation's cause.

William H. Holloman III was eighteen years old in 1942 when he joined the Army Air Corps for pilot training. He trained in Biloxi, Mississippi, and graduated from the now-famous Tuskegee Army Air Field in Alabama. Then he and other Tuskegee airmen flew combat missions over Europe. In this interview conducted by Irv Broughton several decades after the war's end, Holloman recalls the discrimination he and other black pilots faced as they went to serve their country.

A group of Tuskegee airmen receive flight instructions. Tuskegee pilots and other black servicemen faced discrimination during the war.

I think up until high school, I had been giving my parents trouble in school. My father made the comment that my attention span was too short for me to learn how to fly an airplane. He also led me to believe that he did not think I was smart enough—he somewhat ridiculed me about my desire.

What did he say?

Well, he just said, "You don't have what it takes to fly"—or something to that effect. He challenged me. He said, "You don't have the intelligence." He also commented that he had never seen a Negro pilot—that he didn't know if there were any. I told him that I did know two Black pilots, that my squadron leader in the CAP [Civilian Air Patrol] was a pilot as was his replacement. . . .

You know, our city produced a large number of Black airmen during the war. I remember James McCullin, whose mother ran the candy store right on the corner from our school, was the first to sign up for pilot training in St. Louis, Missouri. Another pilot I knew well was Wendell Pruitt, who had completed pilot training before I went in. His brother, Luther, who lived a few doors from us, worked with my cousin. Wendell looked sharp in that uniform, and I was determined to be just like him.

What was the hardest transition to the Tuskegee Institute, when you got there?

My ignorance of racial practices in the south. When I left St. Louis, there were four of us that left together for Keesler Field, Biloxi, Mississippi, on the train. It was a Pullman car and we were in a four-person parlor. We had the freedom of the train from St. Louis to Evansville, Indiana. When the train left Evansville, the conductor came in and told us we had to move to the coach car up front. We explained that our tickets were for this parlor compartment to Mobile, Alabama, and that we had been paid for by the government. John Squires told him we were not going to move. There was much discussion on the matter, and after intervention by some army official, we were permitted to stay put. Sometime after the matter was settled, and before reaching Nashville, Tennessee, we all went to the dining car to eat, as we had done from St. Louis to Evansville. We were refused service. Again, it was pointed out that we had government paid meal tickets and were entitled to eat. At this point, we were told we would have to wait until colored passengers were served. When we returned again, there was this curtain up which they sat us behind for our meal. It was very degrading. We felt apprehension and fear. I told myself anything was worth going through to get an opportunity to fly. After our meal, we were told to stay in our parlor. As I recall, when we arrived at Nashville, Tennessee, the conductor attempted to move us to the Jim Crow car again, and even called for the military police (MP) to force us to move, but they left us there until the next morning at which time they took the Pullman car off the train and informed us that there was no space in the remaining Pullman cars. We were forced to move to the Jim Crow car for Blacks in coach, but were still permitted to go to the dining car, with its curtain, for our meals. I think one of the more depressing things about the whole incident was that our uniforms were nice, clean and neatly pressed when we left St. Louis. We were very proud of the way we looked and that we were embarking on a venture to serve our country. In that Jim Crow car, right behind the engine, believe me it was hot. The windows open and the soot from that engine blew into the car. By the time we got off the train in Biloxi, we looked like death warmed over. You couldn't tell what color those uniforms were. You must understand, here we were, four 18 years-old, and for the first time in our lives we were far away from our parents, friends and home. The excitement of being near military aircraft and the joy of future dreams somewhat offset the disgust and anger of a racist system that required young Black Americans to endure such treatment. At any rate, the trucks picked us up and took us to Keesler Field, Mississippi, where we spent the next three or four weeks.

Do you remember anything unusual about being at Tuskegee?

We were all young kids—many had no college education—which requires us to go through one semester of college at Tuskegee Institute—now Tuskegee University—to prepare us for the strenuous training ahead. We went to school all day and studied half the night for about two months. We were in a college environment, yet we were controlled. By this I mean we had to march everywhere we went, to and from class and mess. . . .

Did you have any friends that didn't make it? It was a demanding experience.

Someone was leaving all the time for failure to keep up with the academic pace or the inability to adjust to the discipline demanded of military personnel. Of the members that were eventually in our CTD [cadet training] class—there were six from St. Louis—only Fischer didn't make it to pre-flight. He remained at the Institute after our class left to begin our first phase of training at Tuskegee Army Air Field. My closest friend was washed back in primary, so the remaining four graduated and went on to fly combat in Italy.

Excerpted from *Forever Remembered: The Fliers of WWII*, by Irv Broughton (Spokane, WA: Eastern Washington University Press, 2001). Copyright © 2001 by Irv Broughton. Reprinted by permission of Eastern Washington University Press.

Chapter 3

War in Europe

lthough all branches of the American military participated in the war against the Japanese, only the navy was active in the European theater in the months following Germany's declaration of war. U.S. destroyers were helping protect the vital shipping lanes between North America and England. It was not until November 1942 that U.S. ground forces became actively involved in the war against Germany and its allies. In that month, American and British forces landed in French-controlled Morocco and Algeria. There, at strategic North African port cities, the American GIs defeated French colonial forces and established bases from which to aid the British army in expelling Axis forces in Libya and Tunisia. With that success, General Dwight D. Eisenhower, commander of the North African landings, sent units into Tunisia to try and trap the German army. The trap failed, and the Americans learned quickly that the German tacticians and their soldiers were not

so easily defeated. It was not until May of the following year that North Africa was cleared of Axis forces.

In July 1943, the Allies began their campaign to take back Europe. U.S., British,

A gun crew on a U.S. destroyer.

and Free French armies invaded the Italian island of Sicily where they faced stiff resistance from Italian and German defenders. But the Allied armies, which had superior naval and air power, eventually overwhelmed the Axis forces. By August, victory was complete, and 135,000 Axis prisoners fell into Allied hands. Both sides, however, had each lost over 31,000 men in the terrible fighting.

In September, the British army in Sicily crossed the Straits of Messina and began a steady advance up the boot of Italy proper. The American army entered Italy as it had

General Dwight D. Eisenhower gives orders to a group of American soldiers.

Sicily, by seaborne invasion. However, the Italian government capitulated before the Americans landed. As a result, the GIs expected only token resistance. But the German forces in Italy had not surrendered and at Salerno, where the Americans came ashore, the Germans put up stiff resistance. A counterattack nearly drove the Americans back into the sea. Allied air power, however, proved to be the saving grace for the trapped American army. After repeated bombings, the German offensive was halted, and soon the British army driving up from the south linked up with the American beachhead. With the lower part of Italy secured, the Allied armies began to push north—the British moving up the eastern edge of Italy and the Americans advancing up the western shore. Progress was slow and costly; the Germans had excellent defensive positions in the hills around Naples and farther north at Monte Cassino. It was not until June 4, 1944, that Rome—barely half way up the Italian peninsula—was liberated. By then a new invasion of Europe was in the works.

The Allies had been waging an air campaign against the industrialized cities of the Rhine and Ruhr valleys in the border region between Germany and France since 1940. By 1942, the British and American commands had devised various plans to invade France and quickly race to capture these vital Nazi resources. It was not until late 1943 that the Allies believed they had sufficient forces and technology to successfully stage Operation Overlord, the code name given

Allied Invasions

Legend:
- Axis occupation
- Allied nations
- Neutral nations
- Major Allied drives
- Major battles

Murmansk

Narvik

Norwegian Sea

SWEDEN

Trondheim

NORWAY

Gulf of Bothnia

FINLAND

North Atlantic Ocean

Oslo

Leningrad

U.S.S.R.

Stockholm

North Sea

Moscow

DENMARK

Baltic Sea

IRELAND

GREAT BRITAIN

Hamburg

NETHERLANDS

London

Antwerp

BELGIUM

Berlin

Warsaw

Kursk
July 1943

Stalingrad

English Channel

Normandy invasion
June 6, 1944

Battle of the Bulge
Dec. 1944

Kiev

Paris

GERMANY

FRANCE

SLOVAKIA

Vienna

HUNGARY

Bay of Biscay

SWITZERLAND

Budapest

ROMANIA

Rhone Valley
invasion

ITALY

YUGOSLAVIA

Black Sea

BULGARIA

IRAN

PORTUGAL

Madrid

SPAIN

Rome

Cassino
Nov. 1943

ALBANIA

TURKEY

Tyrrhenian Sea

Adriatic Sea

GREECE

Anzio
Jan. 1944

Salerno
Sept. 1943

Ionian Sea

Aegean Sea

SYRIA

Mediterranean Sea

Athens

CYPRUS

LEBANON

IRAQ

Oran

Algiers

Tunis

SICILY

Sicily invaded
July-August 1943

CRETE

PALESTINE

TRANSJORDAN

Casablanca

MOROCCO

ALGERIA

TUNISIA

Kasserine Pass
Feb. 1943

Tripoli

Benghazi

Cairo

SAUDI ARABIA

EGYPT

LIBYA

Scale of Miles
500

to the invasion of northern France. At the Teheran conference between Russia, Britain, and the United States, President Roosevelt and Prime Minister Churchill informed their Soviet counterpart, Joseph Stalin, that in spring 1944 a cross-channel invasion would open a second front in Europe. On June 6, 1944, Operation Overlord began. An invasion force made up mainly of British, American, and Canadian troops crossed the English Channel and stormed ashore in the Normandy region of France. Securing five beachheads was the first objective. These were all defended by German pillboxes—small low concrete emplacements for weapons, minefields, and thousands of garrison troops. The British and Canadian forces at Gold, Sword, and Juno beaches, as well as the Americans at Utah Beach, made good headway, but the American soldiers at Omaha Beach met stiff resistance from a German division. Still, by nightfall, 155,000 men had landed and secured the Allied beachhead. The liberation of France had begun.

Between June 1944 and May 1945, the Allied armies in the west and the Soviet armies in the east trapped Adolf Hitler's Third Reich. The German defenders were not easily overcome. Years of warfare had made them a deadly and experienced foe. The Nazis were committed enough to stage a counterattack against the overwhelming Allied armies on the western front in the winter of 1944. But the number of men, planes, tanks, and other weapons of war at Allied disposal far outweighed that of the Germans. When the factories of the Rhineland fell to the British and Americans in March and April 1945, the war's outcome was foretold. On May 2, Russian forces on the eastern front seized Berlin only to learn Hitler had committed suicide days before. With Hitler dead, German officials surrendered to a joint delegation of American, British, and Soviet officials on May 7, 1945. The long fight against Nazi aggression had ended, but World War II was still not over. The forces of Japan were still fighting hard in the Pacific theater, and American efforts were now turned solely upon defeating this last opposition.

Operation Torch

Before the Allies set their sights on retaking Europe from the Nazis, they decided upon an invasion of North Africa to rid that continent of the Axis powers. In November 1942, American troops staged an amphibious assault, known as Operation Torch, upon French Morocco. One objective of the invasion was the port of Oran. Here, as at other landing points, French forces—whose new government had agreed to repel all invasions of French soil—opposed the Allies.

Leo Disher was a United Press correspondent aboard the U.S. Coast Guard cutter, the Walney. *Disher had recently broken his ankle and was on crutches as the ship moved into Oran harbor. The* Walney *came under steady fire as it entered the harbor and Disher was wounded in the ensuing action. The French put up a strong if brief defense. Most of the colonials were not committed to fighting Americans, especially since it was obvious that the Allies meant to defeat Hitler and eventually liberate France. Still, as Disher relates, the defenders claimed a lot of lives at Oran.*

I made my way from the stern toward the bridge. . . .

My crutches had begun to wedge painfully into my arm pits and my right leg was becoming exceedingly weary. To ease it,

I braced the crutches across the passageway and leaning on them with my forearms, rested by pushing hard with my back against the bulkhead. From that position I could see, across the twenty feet of the bridge, the high bulk of cliffs, now very near. We were running parallel to them, heading westward. Ahead now I saw the gleam of scattered lights.

It was Oran.

We became silent on the bridge. There was no sound anywhere except the constant swish of the water against the ship's plates.

Then a searchlight blazed. . . .

And then came a stream of bullets.

Flaming tracer lead arched out lazily before the ship. And then the sound of stuttering machine guns. Heavy crashes came from the shore and the *Walney* shook. A moment later she shook again. We were being hit with cannon. . . .

[*Commander*] Meyrick passed an order to the men below:

U.S. soldiers aid a fellow serviceman after his ship is sunk off the coast of North Africa by Nazi planes.

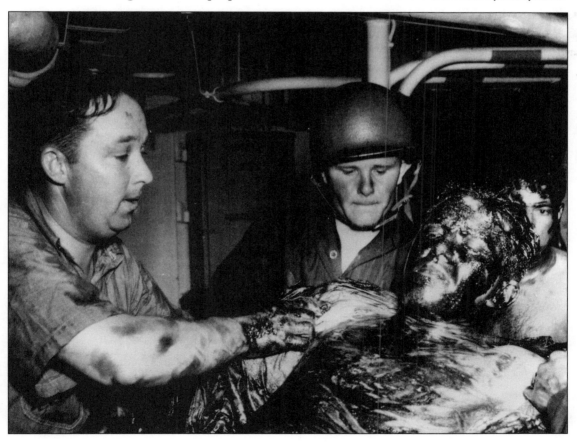

"Lie flat for crash. We are approaching the boom [a barrier to protect the harbor]."

We braced ourselves against the devilish symphony of machine-gun and artillery fire. Our tommy guns began talking back.

Shells and bullets crashed into us, and almost as the *Walney* shuddered with the impact, she snapped the boom. We were through. It had been as easy as that. . . .

Our chief of staff took his hands off the butts of his six-shooters, gripped the loudspeaker microphone and began talking to the French on shore in their own language. He even spoke French with an American accent. "Cease firing," he said. "We are your friends. We are Americans. Cease firing."

It seemed to me then that all hell broke loose around us. We were hit time and again. The chief of staff was a brave man. His voice went on amid the awful noise of battle until he fell against the microphone with his six-shooters still unfired in their holsters.

Everything was happening at once. The officer below decks began directing American assault troops to midships, where they were partially screened by the superstructure as they went over the side. A shell hit one of our fuel drums, spreading liquid fire along the deck. A destroyer loomed in front of us. We tried to ram but missed, and there was a savage burst of fire from its guns at almost muzzle-end range. The bridge was raked and raked again.

A French cruiser began firing, too, and then a submarine on our port side opened up. My crutches were knocked away in the first crush of falling men. I fell and crawled to the outside wing bridge in an attempt to see. Shell bursts wounded me in both legs. The *Walney* caught fire below deck. . . .

"Okay!" shouted Lieutenant Cole. "Everybody get off! Get ashore!" Somewhere below our depth charges began exploding. "Everybody ashore!" Our ammunition began blowing up. . . .

In the darkness bodies had fallen against me; and the bodies had risen and fallen again and again. I had somehow lived through it so far. . . .

In the first deluge of fire I lived possibly because I was crawling. The first concussion of shells caught me and tossed me. The blasts were so loud they hurt and seemed solid.

I was tossed . . . and I crawled. I pulled up . . . was hurled down. . . .

I dropped to my knees again and began crawling behind the bridge toward the port ladders. I reached them. They were swept by flame, but I went down. I went down one, then the other. I was on the main deck. Pushing my helmet from my head, I toppled through a shell-torn gap in the rail to the water.

I almost drowned.

The life-tube on my chest had been burst by shrapnel. The one John Cole had tied to my leg was still intact, and my leg floated, while my head stayed below water. Struggling and choking, I pulled at the tube, finally tearing it loose. I began swimming away from the ship while bullets and bits of metal rained down on the water.

Somehow I was not hit. Foot by foot, I swam on, conscious now of pain in my legs. . . .

With infinite weariness I swam into the blackness between a lurching merchant ship and the pier. My eyes closed. My fingers clawed water. I touched a rope and discovered I was again determined to live. I hauled myself up until I got my elbows over the pier rim. Then the full weight of the cast on my leg caught me and I knew I couldn't make it. Slowly and painfully I began losing my grip. Then a single hand groped down and braced me. I swung my good leg up and it caught. Then the hand from above began to pull, and I rolled over the edge with open, gasping mouth pressed against the stone surface of the pier. I could see the man who had pulled me up as a hazy, unreal figure swaying near me. But I saw enough. He had used only one hand because the other had been shot away. I never knew his name, never even knew his nationality, because just then a bullet struck my injured foot. Another bullet later hit the wall and bounced into my temple. I was crawling, sprawling into the dirt, crawling again. . . .

Finally, a French soldier took me over his back like a sack of meal and carried me into a hole in the cliffs. The hole led on, became a corridor, then a system of corridors. . . .

In the long hospital ward, a French nurse stuck a cigarette between my lips and a doctor found a total of twenty-six assorted holes in me. I tried to sleep but the hospital shuddered to the roar of big guns.

In the next bed the American soldier who had helped carry me woke up and grinned. "Ain't it," he asked, "a helluva day?"

Excerpted from *Springboard to Berlin,* by John A. Paris and Ned Russell in collaboration with Leo Disher and Phil Ault (New York, NY: Thomas Y. Crowell, 1943). Copyright © 1943 by Thomas Y. Crowell Company. Reprinted with permission.

Costly Daylight Raids

The American Eighth Air Force flew its first bombing missions over Germany in August 1942. The British tried to persuade the Americans to restrict their flights to nighttime missions to cut down on losses from enemy aircraft and antiaircraft fire. The Americans, however, believed in the accuracy of daylight raids. They had confidence that their bombers—especially the fast and heavily armed B-17s—could make the flights with minimal losses.

However, the American bomber crews suffered terribly at the hands of the German fighter planes. Ten to 20 percent losses were not uncommon. Still, the Allied bombing campaign was taking its toll on German manufacturing and other industries. In 1943, the Eighth Air Force was given the task of destroying the German Messerschmitt airplane factory at Regensburg. Of the 146 B-17s that took off from England, 24 never returned home. Lieutenant Colonel Beirne Lay Jr. was a copilot in one of the surviving B-17s. In this account of the costly raid, he describes what it was like to be hounded by German fighters.

The fear was unpleasant, but it was bearable. I knew that I was going to die, and so were a lot of others. . . .

A few minutes later we absorbed the first wave of a hailstorm of individual fighter

B-17s from the Eighth Air Force drop bombs on Germany in 1942.

attacks that were to engulf us clear to the target in such a blizzard of bullets and shells that a chronological account is difficult. It was at 10:41, over Eupen, that I looked out the window after a minute's lull, and saw two whole squadrons, twelve Me-109's and eleven FW-190's climbing parallel to us as though they were on a steep escalator. The first squadron had reached our level and was pulling ahead to turn into us. The second was not far behind. Several thousand feet below us were many more fighters, their noses cocked up in a maximum climb. Over the interphone came reports of an equal number of enemy aircraft deploying on the other side of the formation. . . .

Swinging their yellow noses around in a wide U turn, the twelve-ship squadron of

Me-109's came in from twelve to two o'clock in pairs. The main event was on. I fought an impulse to close my eyes, and overcame it. . . .

A B-17 turned gradually out of the formation to the right, maintaining altitude. In a split second it completely vanished in a brilliant explosion, from which the only remains were four balls of fire, the fuel tanks, which were quickly consumed as they fell earthward.

I saw blue, red, yellow and aluminum-colored fighters. Their tactics were running fairly true to form, with frontal attacks hitting the low squadron and rear attackers going for the lead and high squadrons. . . .

The manner of the assaults indicated that the pilots knew where we were going and were inspired with a fanatical determination to stop us before we got there. Many pressed attacks home to 250 yards or less, or bolted right through the formation wide out, firing long twenty-second bursts, often presenting point-blank targets on the breakaway. Some committed the fatal error of pulling up instead of going down and out. More experienced pilots came in on frontal attacks with a noticeably slower rate of closure, apparently throttled back, obtaining greater accuracy. But no tactics could halt the close-knit juggernauts of our Fortresses, nor save the single-seaters from paying a terrible price.

Our airplane was endangered by various debris. Emergency hatches, exit doors, prematurely opened parachutes, bodies and assorted fragments of B-17's and Hun fighters breezed past us in the slip stream.

I watched two fighters explode not far beneath, disappear in sheets of orange flame; B-17's dropping out in every stage of distress, from engines on fire to controls shot away; friendly and enemy parachutes floating down, and, on the green carpet far below us, funeral pyres of smoke from fallen fighters, marking our trail.

On we flew through the cluttered wake of a desperate air battle, where disintegrating aircraft were commonplace and the white dots of sixty parachutes in the air at one time were hardly worth a second look. . . .

I looked forward and almost ducked as I watched the tail gunner of a B-17 ahead of us take a bead right on our windshield and cut loose with a stream of tracers that missed us by a few feet as he fired on a fighter attacking us from six o'clock low. I almost ducked again when our own top-turret gunner's twin muzzles pounded away a foot above my head in the full forward position, giving a realistic imitation of cannon shells exploding in the cockpit, while I gave an even better imitation of a man jumping six inches out of his seat.

Still no letup. The fighters queued up like a bread line and let us have it. Each second of time had a cannon shell in it. The strain of being a clay duck in the wrong end of that aerial shooting gallery became almost intolerable.

Near the initial point, at 11:50, one hour and a half after the first of at least 200 individual fighter attacks, the pressure eased off, although hostiles were still in the vicinity. . . .

And then our weary, battered column, short twenty-four bombers, but still holding the close formation that had brought the remainder through by sheer air discipline and gunnery, turned in to the target. I knew that our bombardiers were grim as death while they synchronized their sights on the great Me-109 shops lying below us in a curve of the winding blue Danube, close to the outskirts of Regensburg. Our B-17 gave a slight lift and a red light went out on the instrument panel. Our bombs were away. We turned from the target toward the snow-capped

Alps. I looked back and saw a beautiful sight—a rectangular pillar of smoke rising from the Me-109 plant.

Going Ashore at Salerno

The retaking of Europe by the Allied armies began with the invasion of Italy in 1943. In July of that year, American and British units assaulted the island of Sicily. Then in September, the U.S. Fifth Army under General Mark Clark staged an amphibious invasion of Italy proper, establishing a beachhead near the city of Salerno. On September 9, Allied warships opened fire to prepare the way for the landing craft streaming toward the beaches at Salerno. The fighting was vicious as the U.S. infantrymen—once landed—had to pick their way through barbed wire and mines while dodging fire from enemy machine guns and powerful 88 mm antitank guns.

John Steinbeck, the famed author of The Grapes of Wrath, *was a war correspondent for the* New York Times *syndicate in 1943. He went ashore with the Fifth Army at Salerno and reported what he saw and heard. In this article, Steinbeck describes a one-sided conversation he had with a soldier of one of the first landings.*

Somewhere in the Mediterranean Theater.—There is a good beach at Salerno, and a very good landing at Red Beach No. 2. The ducks [amphibious trucks] were coming loaded ashore and running up out of the water and joining the lines of trucks, and the pontoon piers were out in the water with large landing cars up against them. Along the beach the bulldozers were at work pushing up sand ramps for the trucks to land on and just back of the beach were the white tapes that mean land mines have not been cleared out.

There are little bushes on the sand dunes at Red Beach south of the Sele River, and in a hole in the sand buttressed by sand bags a soldier sat with a leather covered steel telephone beside him. His shirt was off and his back was dark with sunburn. His helmet lay in the bottom of the hole and his rifle was on a little pile of brush to keep the sand out of it. He had staked a shelter half on a pole to shade him from the sun, and he had spread bushes on top of that to camouflage it. Beside him was a water can and an empty "C" ration can to drink out of.

The soldier said, "Sure you can have a drink. Here, I'll pour it for you." He tilted the water can over the tin cup. "I hate to tell you what it tastes like," he said. I took a drink. "Well, doesn't it?" he said. "It sure does," I said. Up in the hills the 88's were popping and the little bursts threw sand about where they hit, and off to the seaward our cruisers were popping away at the 88's in the hills.

The soldier slapped at a sand fly on his shoulder and then scratched the place where it had bitten him. His face was dirty and streaked where the sweat had run down through the dirt, and his hair and his eyebrows were sunburned almost white. But there was a kind of gayety about him. His telephone buzzed and he answered it, and said, "Hasn't come through yet, sir, no sir. I'll tell him." He clicked off the phone.

"When'd you come ashore?" he asked. And then without waiting for an answer he went on. "I came in just before dawn yesterday. I wasn't with the very first, but right in the second." He seemed to be very glad about it. "It was hell," he said, "it was bloody hell." He seemed to be gratified at the hell it was, and that was right. The great question had been solved for him. He had been under fire. He knew now what he would do under fire. He would never have to go through that uncertainty again. "I got pretty near up

An American ship explodes after being hit by German bombers off the coast of Sicily.

to there," he said, and pointed to two beautiful Greek temples about a mile away. "And then I got sent back here for beach communications. When did you say you got ashore?" and again he didn't wait for an answer.

"It was dark as hell," he said, "and we were just waiting out there." He pointed to the sea where the mass of the invasion fleet rested. "If we thought we were going to sneak ashore we were nuts," he said. "They were waiting for us all fixed up. Why, I heard they had been here two weeks waiting for us. They knew just where we were going to land. They had machine guns in the sand dunes and 88's on the hills.

"We were out there all packed in an L.C.I. [landing craft] and then the hell broke loose. The sky was full of it and the star shells lighted it up and the tracers crisscrossed and the noise—we saw the assault go in, and then one of them hit a surf mine and went up, and in the light you could see them go flying about. I could see the boats land and the guys go wiggling and running, and then maybe there'd be a lot of white lines and some of them would waddle about and collapse and some would hit the beach.

"It didn't seem like men getting killed, more like a picture, like a moving picture. We were pretty crowded up in there though, and then all of a sudden it came on me that this wasn't a moving picture. Those were guys getting the hell shot out of them, and then I got kind of scared, but what I

wanted to do mostly was move around. I didn't like being cooped up there where you couldn't get away or get down close to the ground.

"Well the firing would stop and then it would get pitch black even then, and it was just beginning to get light too but the 88's sort of winked on the hills like messages, and the shells were bursting all around us. They had lots of 88's and they shot at everything. I was just getting real scared when we got the order to move in, and I swear that is the longest trip I ever took, that mile to the beach. I thought we'd never get there. I figured that if I was only on the beach I could dig down and get out of the way. There was too damn many of us there in that L.C.I. I wanted to spread out. That one that hit the mine was still burning when we went on by it. Then we bumped the beach and the ramps went down and I hit the water up to my waist.

"The minute I was on the beach I felt better. It didn't seem like everybody was shooting at me, and I got up to that line of brush and flopped down and some other guys flopped down beside me and then we got feeling a little foolish. We stood up and moved on. Didn't say anything to each other, we just moved on. It was coming daylight then and the flashes of the guns weren't so bright. I felt a little like I was drunk. The ground heaved around under my feet and I was dull. I guess that was because of the firing. My ears aren't so good yet. I guess we moved up too far because I got sent back here." He laughed openly. "I

War correspondent Ernie Pyle (center) chats with American general George Patton (left) and another serviceman.

might have gone on right into Rome if some one hadn't sent me back. I guess I might have walked right up that hill there."

The cruisers began firing on the hill and the 88's fired back. From over near the hill came the heavy thudding of .50-caliber machine guns. The soldier felt pretty good. He knew what he could do now. He said, "When did you say you came ashore?"

Excerpted from *Once There Was a War,* by John Steinbeck (New York, NY: Viking, 1958). Copyright © 1958 by John Steinbeck. Reprinted by permission of Viking Penguin, a division of Penguin Books, USA, Inc.

The Death of Captain Waskow

Ernie Pyle was one of the most respected correspondents of World War II. An ace reporter,

Pyle knew of the larger strategic issues of the war but seldom wrote about them. Instead, his dispatches were filled with the gritty details of the soldiers' war, and the GIs loved him for conveying what he called a "worm's eye view of the war." His style was admired by more than just the soldiers, however, for Pyle was awarded the Pulitzer Prize for journalism in 1944.

Pyle began his war reporting in England, then moved with the Allied armies as they invaded North Africa, Sicily, and Italy. In one of his articles, dated January 10, 1944, Pyle describes the effect the death of a beloved captain has on his comrades during the fighting in the hill country around Naples, Italy. The somber mood of his report brought the soldiers' anguish home to readers in the States.

Pyle went on to report on the invasion of France and then was sent to the Pacific theater. There, as the marines stormed the tiny island of Ie Shima (near Okinawa), Pyle was struck dead by a Japanese sniper's bullet.

At the front lines in Italy, January 10, 1944—In this war I have known a lot of officers who were loved and respected by the soldiers under them. But never have I crossed the trail of any man as beloved as Capt. Henry T. Waskow of Belton, Texas.

Capt. Waskow was a company commander in the 36th Division. He had led his company since long before it left the [United] States. He was very young, only in his middle twenties, but he carried in him a sincerity and gentleness that made people want to be guided by him.

"After my own father, he came next," a sergeant told me.

"He always looked after us," a soldier said. "He'd go to bat for us every time." . . .

I was at the foot of the mule trail the night they brought Capt. Waskow's body down. The moon was nearly full at the time, and you could see far up the trail, and even part way across the valley below. . . .

Dead men had been coming down the mountain all evening, lashed onto the backs of mules. They came lying belly-down across the wooden pack-saddles, their heads hanging down on the left side of the mule, their stiffened legs sticking out awkwardly from the other side, bobbing up and down as the mule walked. . . .

The first one came early in the morning. They slid him down from the mule and stood him on his feet for a moment, while they got a new grip. In the half light he might have been merely a sick man standing there, leaning on the others. Then they laid him on the ground in the shadow of the low stone wall alongside the road.

I don't know who that first one was. You feel small in the presence of dead men, and ashamed at being alive, and you don't ask silly questions.

We left him there beside the road, that first one, and we all went back into the cowshed and sat on water cans or lay on the straw, waiting for the next batch of mules. . . .

Then a soldier came into the cowshed and said there were some more bodies outside. We went out into the road. Four mules stood there, in the moonlight, in the road where the trail came down off the mountain. The soldiers who led them stood there waiting. "This one is Captain Waskow," one of them said quietly.

Two men unlashed his body from the mule and lifted it off and laid it in the shadow beside the low stone wall. Other men took the other bodies off. Finally there were five lying end to end in a long row, alongside the road. You don't cover up dead men in the combat zone. They just lie there in the shadows until somebody else comes after them.

The unburdened mules moved off to their olive orchard. The men in the road seemed reluctant to leave. They stood around, and gradually one by one I could sense them moving closer to Capt. Waskow's body. Not so much to look, I think, as to say something in finality to him, and to themselves. I stood close by and I could hear.

One soldier came and looked down, and he said out loud, "God damn it." That's all he said, and then he walked away. Another one came. He said, "God damn it to hell anyway." He looked down for a few last moments, and then he turned and left.

Another man came; I think he was an officer. It was hard to tell . . . in the half light, for [everyone was] bearded and grimy dirty. The man looked down into the dead captain's face, and then he spoke directly to him, as though he were alive. He said: "I'm sorry, old man."

Then a soldier came and stood beside the officer, and bent over, and he too spoke to his dead captain, not in a whisper but awfully tenderly, and he said:

"I sure am sorry, sir."

Then the first man squatted down, and he reached down and took the dead hand, and he sat there for a full five minutes, holding the dead hand in his own and looking intently into the dead face, and he never uttered a sound all the time he sat there.

And finally he put the hand down, and then reached up and gently straightened the points of the captain's shirt collar, and then he sort of rearranged the tattered edges of his uniform around the wound. And then he got up and walked away down the road in the moonlight, all alone.

Excerpted from "The Death of Captain Waskow," by Ernie Pyle, January 10, 1944. Copyright © 1944 by Scripps Howard. Reprinted with permission.

The Subject of Conversation Is Women

Irwin Shaw was a playwright and short-story writer. He had written a well-received antiwar play called Bury the Dead *in 1936. When World War II erupted, Shaw joined the league of American war journalists and covered the war for both* Stars and Stripes *and* Yank. *In 1943, while reporting for* Stars and Stripes *on the Mediterranean theater, Shaw made an informal survey of American troops to find out their favorite topic of conversation. The results surprised no one but did provide a humorous diversion from the horrors of war.*

The people back home are very interested in hearing what soldiers talk about, and when I came over here I resolved to send back accurate reports on what the army says in bivouac, on leave, and in the front lines. I'm not so sure that's entirely possible any more.

I've been at all the airfields between Miami and Cairo and I've talked to hundreds of soldiers on the long road between Egypt and Algiers. I don't think you'd want to print the ordinary conversations among GI's.

Aside from the richness of the language, army conversation has a beautiful simplicity and directness. It is all on one solid everlasting subject . . . Women. This makes it different from the talk about women and baseball.

Occasionally a soldier will deviate a little and his control will leave him, like a pitcher tiring in the late innings, and he will talk about frivolous things like what he did when his company was cut off by the Jerries and what he thinks ought to be done with Germany after the war. But very soon he will suddenly catch himself and start talking about the blonde girl he knew back at Purdue who measured thirty-seven and three-quarter inches around the chest, so help him God.

In Puerto Rico, where my plane stopped for a few hours, the first thing I was told was that the food was good and there was plenty of girls if you knew Spanish.

In Khartoum, where I slept on the same porch with a Liberator crew, the tail gunner was talking about his wife who was in Chicago.

"Chicago," the radio operator said. "That's a hell of a place to leave a wife."

"The Great Lakes Naval Training Station is in Chicago," the top turret gunner said dreamily. "There are 5,000,000 sailors in Chicago."

"That's all right," the tail gunner said grimly. "Every couple of weeks I send home a fifty calibre machine-gun bullet. My wife puts them on the mantelpiece to remind those sailors her husband's a gunner. She ain't had no trouble yet."

In Cairo a young British Hurricane pilot who had lived in America, talked for a whole night about how he was going to buy a house on the top of Lookout Mountain in Hollywood after the war, and live there with his wife and produce five children. After a long while I got him to admit that he had personally sunk a four thousand ton freighter in the English Channel.

A French private who travelled with me for a whole day, returning to his unit, which had granted him ten days' leave in which to get married in Constantine, merely said, *"Je suis très fatigué* [I am very tired]," and nothing more.

In Algiers the conversation about fair sex has a severely practical turn. The men watch the pretty girls going by in their pretty dresses, and they sigh and turn to the newcomer and say, "It is necessary to know French."

I suppose there are a few fellows somewhere who spend all their spare time talking about Clausewitz's theories and the war aims of the Allies, but I haven't found them yet.

Does anybody want to hear about the Swedish girl I met in Madison, Wisconsin, in 1939 . . . ?

Excerpted from *Stars and Stripes*, Africa edition, June 19, 1943.

A Hero at Anzio

As the Italian campaign bogged down in the hills outside Naples, the Allies planned to attack the strong German positions by staging an amphibi-

American soldiers fire across enemy lines in Italy, 1944.

ous assault behind enemy lines. In January 1944, two allied divisions landed at the resort towns of Anzio and Nettuno with little opposition. But the Germans reacted quickly and used tanks and airpower to counterattack the Allied beachhead. The fighting was fierce as the British and American divisions were nearly driven back into the sea. Only through stubborn persistence did the Allied lines hold.

A New York Herald Tribune *war correspondent, Homer Bigart, was amongst the American troops who suffered through the German counterattack. In this article from February 20, Bigart relates the tale of one artillery observer who is faced with a grave decision as the Germans overrun his position. Bigart's story captures both the desperation and heroism that marked the Anzio campaign. Yet, despite the tenacity of the Allies, the invasion did little to help their progress through the Italian highlands. In the end, the Anzio campaign was a costly failure.*

With the 5th Army on Anzio Beach Head, Italy (Delayed)—A young American artillery observer, finding himself surrounded by German infantry in today's fluid fighting southeast of Carroceto (Aprilla), performed the highest act of heroism possible for a field artilleryman. He ordered a barrage put down on his own position—a farmhouse which was being overrun by enemy troops.

In a steady, quiet voice, this twenty-four-year-old lieutenant, a former Mid-West school teacher, gave by telephone the coordinates of the yellow concrete farmhouse from which he had observed and reported a German advance. At the other end of the wire Captain Harry C. Lane, of Tulsa, Oklahoma, protested, but the voice said firmly: "What difference does it make? Go ahead and shoot."

A moment later shells from twenty howitzers crashed down upon the farmhouse and surrounding area. The telephone went dead.

It was assumed that the lieutenant either was killed by the barrage or was taken prisoner by the Germans, who, despite heavy losses, remained in control of the area. He had been warned at dawn by Major Franklin T. Gardner, of Tulsa, that the Allied outpost line probably could not withstand another attack. He was told that when the infantry retired to new defensive positions he should fall back with them.

But the lieutenant had won the Silver Star in December by staying after infantry had fled. In that action near Venafro, he called for fire on his own position. The barrage killed scores of Germans and broke up their counter-attacks. The lieutenant came out uninjured, and possibly he figured today that he could do it again.

So, when the Germans began their infiltration tactics the lieutenant kept lowering the range of Allied guns until the heavy howitzer shells were bursting a few hundred yards in front of the farmhouse. His protecting screen of infantry began to retreat and the lieutenant sent his own men back with them. They took the radio, leaving him alone with a telephone.

For thirty minutes the lieutenant continued to adjust two fire missions—on the Germans approaching the farmhouse and on another enemy group just beyond. Then the Germans closed in. The lieutenant adjusted the fire first to the right of the farmhouse, then to the left. He told Captain Lane that he was burning his codes. Then he said: "All right, pour it on."

Excerpted from *Herald Tribune*, by Homer Bigart, February 20, 1944. Copyright © 1944 by the New York Herald Tribune. Reprinted by permission of Center for American History.

The Great Crusade

On June 6, 1944, American, British, and Canadian armies stormed the beaches of Normandy to begin the task of retaking France. The invasion required months of preparation, but relied on the will of the troops to carry it through. The overall command of Operation Overlord, as it was called, was given to American general Dwight D. Eisenhower. On the morning of the invasion, Eisenhower addressed the servicemen who were assigned the historic undertaking. Recognizing the campaign would not only secure France but also give the Allies a route into Germany, Eisenhower told his men that they were embarking on a Great Crusade to free Europe once and for all of the Nazi menace.

Soldiers, Sailors and Airmen of the Allied Expeditionary Forces: You are about to embark upon the Great Crusade, toward which we have striven these many months. The eyes of the world are upon you. The hopes and prayers of liberty-loving people everywhere march with you. In company with our brave Allies and brothers-in-arms on other Fronts you will bring about the destruction of the German war machine, the elimination of Nazi tyranny over oppressed peoples of Europe, and security for ourselves in a free world.

Your task will not be an easy one. Your enemy is well trained, well equipped and battle-hardened. He will fight savagely.

But this is the year 1944! Much has happened since the Nazi triumphs of 1940–41. The United Nations have inflicted upon the Germans great defeats, in open battle, man-to-man. Our air offensive has seriously reduced their strength in the air and their capacity to wage war on the ground. Our Home Fronts have given us an overwhelm-

ing superiority in weapons and munitions of war, and placed at our disposal great reserves of trained fighting men. The tide has turned! The free men of the world are marching together to Victory!

I have full confidence in your courage, devotion to duty and skill in battle. We will accept nothing less than full victory!

Good Luck! And let us all beseech the blessing of Almighty God upon this great and noble undertaking.

Excerpted from Dwight D. Eisenhower's address "The Great Crusade," June 6, 1944.

"If We're Going to Die, Let's Die up There"

Warren Rulien was a soldier in the Sixteenth Infantry Regiment that went ashore on the western half of Omaha Beach on June 6, 1944. Omaha was one of two landing sites for American troops on D-Day and was by far the bloodiest of the five Allied beachheads. Omaha's defenses had not been damaged by the early morning bombing raids, and the naval fire targeted at Omaha had done little. In addition, Omaha was held by a veteran German infantry division and not the second-rate soldiers who held the other beaches.

In an interview several decades later, Warren Rulien recalls what it was like hitting the beaches on that fateful day. As Rulien remembers, most of the first troops off the landing craft were cut down before making it to the beach. Pinned down by German machine-gun and artillery fire, the survivors huddled behind anything that could provide cover. Only after a few brave leaders took

charge, did the weary foot soldiers begin to fight their way inland.

American soldiers approach the beach at Normandy, France.

"Eight rope nets had been hung over the side of the ship and we began climbing down into the landing crafts. This wasn't an easy thing to do with all the equipment you had on and the rifle. Waves from the English Channel would separate the landing craft from the side of the ship and then it would crash back against the hull. I got down near the bottom of the net and had to time my jump into the landing craft.

"I felt so rotten from the seasickness that I was half enthusiastic about hitting the shore just to get off that landing craft. As we got nearer to the shore, bullets began hitting the sides but could not penetrate. . . . We ducked down low. It wasn't long after we stopped when the front of the landing craft was lowered. For a few seconds, everything seemed quiet and nobody moved. The image that flashed through my mind was 'They can shoot us through the front of the craft.'

"Someone shouted, 'Let's go!' We began pouring out of the craft, and as I stepped off of the ramp, I dropped into water up to my chest and I lost my rifle and began wading in to shore.

"On both sides of me were many soldiers coming from other landing crafts, all wading in to shore. In front of me were steel rails driven into the bottom of the sea, which extended six feet out of the water, and on top were mines. By the time I got to the steel rails, the water was up to my waist. There were many dead soldiers floating around in the water, and bullets began hitting only a few feet in front of me, so I stepped behind one of the steel rails and squatted down. A young replacement about nineteen years old that was from my platoon shouted at me, 'Hey, Rulien, here I go!' and began running toward shore. He stepped onto the sandbar, and machine-gun fire opened up, and he dropped into the water on the other side.

"I took one of the bodies that was floating in the water and pushed it in front of me toward the shore. I had only gone a short distance when three or four soldiers began lining up behind me. I stood up and shouted, 'Don't bunch up!' and walked off, leaving them with the body. I got down as low as I could in the water until I reached the sandbar, and then I crossed it on my belly and kept moving forward until I reached the beach, where soldiers were bunched-up behind a sandbank.

"Lying beside me, on his back, was a soldier who had been shot in the stomach. He held his hand over his stomach, moaning, but only for a short time; then he died. I picked up his rifle, threw back the bolt, and looked down the barrel to make sure that sand hadn't been jammed into the barrel. I put a clip of ammunition in and looked up the hill and saw German soldiers running along the crest. At that distance, they looked about two inches high and I began firing at them. On the shore, there were officers sitting there, stunned. Nobody was taking command. Landing crafts were continuing to bring waves of soldiers in, and they were bunching up on the beach.

"Finally, out on the water, coming towards the shore, walking straight up with a staff of officers with him, I recognized Colonel Taylor, regimental commander. He stepped across the sandbar and bullets began hitting the water around him. He laid down on his stomach and started crawling towards shore, and when he got in, I heard him say to the officers, 'If we're going to die, let's die up there.' It seemed to take effect, because the officers began moving their men from that two yards of beach to reach their objective."

Excerpted from *Voices of D-Day: The Story of the Allied Invasion Told by Those Who Were There*, edited by Ronald J. Drez (Baton Rouge, LA, Louisiana State University Press, 1996). Copyright © 1996 by Louisiana State University Press. Reprinted with permission.

Bravery and Gallantry Beyond Belief

The American divisions landing at Omaha Beach on June 6, 1944, would face obstacles not present at other D-Day invasion beaches. Most noticeably, the terrain at Omaha was not ideal for an amphibious assault. Sheer cliffs bordered the sandy shoreline, providing the Germans with strategic positions for pillboxes and bunkers. The American troops streaming ashore would be subjected to gunfire from all sides and would have almost no place to hide.

The inexperienced men of the 116th Infantry Regiment were given the task of taking the high ground on the right side of the Omaha beachhead. Stumbling ashore under constant fire, the soldiers found their mission was not easily executed. With comrades falling all around them, lucky soldiers like Sergeant Warner Hamlett ran to a low seawall just beyond the sandy strip. As Hamlett remembers in an interview conducted years later, it was obvious to most of the survivors that they could not stay at the seawall forever. Resisting the urge to hide, the men—a few

soldiers at a time—eventually moved forward to knock out the German defenses.

"As the boat made the run for the beach, the lieutenant went to each man and patted them on the back and told them, 'Go get them rascals!'

"After we jumped into the water, it was every man for himself. I waded parallel to the beach with my squad because the heavy fire was directed towards the boats. As I was going straight towards the beach, I saw Lieutenant Hilscher go down on his knees

German pillboxes, like the one pictured here, at Omaha Beach made the Allied landing difficult and deadly.

as a shell exploded. He fell into the hole caused by the explosion. He died there on the beach. Lieutenant Hilscher was from Texas.

"When I finally reached the edge of the water, I started to run towards the seawall under a deafening roar of explosions and bullets. I saw a hole about seventy-five feet away, so I ran and jumped in, landing on top of O.T. Grimes [another soldier] As soon as I caught my breath, I dashed forward again, but had to stop between the obstacles in order to rest. The weight of wet clothes, sand, and equipment made it difficult to run. One of the South Boston soldiers, Mervin L. Matze, had run straight to the seawall and was motioning for us to come on. At the same time, he was yelling, 'Get off the beach!' Our only chance was to get off the beach as quick as possible, because there we were sitting ducks. While resting in between the obstacles, Private Gillingham fell beside me, white with fear. He seemed to be begging for help with his eyes. His look was that of a child asking what to do. I said, 'Gillingham, let's stay separated as much as we can, because the Germans will fire at two quicker than one.' He remained silent and then I heard a shell coming and dove into the sand facedown. Shrapnel rose over my head and hit all around me. It took Gillingham's chin off, including the bone, except for a small piece of flesh. He tried to hold his chin in place as he ran towards the seawall. He made it to the wall, where Will Hawks and I gave him his morphine shot. He stayed with me for approximately thirty minutes until he died. The entire time, he remained conscious and aware that he was dying.

"We were supposed to wait at the seawall until wire cutters could cut the tremendous web of wire that the Germans had placed on top of it. During this time, Lieutenant Wise of F Company was directing his team behind the seawall, when a bullet hit him in the forehead. He continued to instruct his men until he sat down and held his head in the palm of his hand before falling over dead.

"We waited at the seawall until time to cross over the path cleared by the wire cutters. As we crossed the seawall, Germans in pillboxes fired upon each man as he dashed forward. After we crossed, the ground provided more protection, with small bushes and gullies. We took time to reorganize and planned to knock out the pillbox. First we tried direct attack using TNT on the end of long poles, but this was impossible because the Germans could shoot the men down as soon as they saw them coming through the barbed wire strung in front of the pillboxes. We then decided to run between the pillboxes and enter the trenches that connected them. These trenches had been dug by the Germans and gave them mobility and a means of escape. We entered the trenches, slipped behind the pillboxes, and threw grenades into them. After the explosion, we ran into the boxes to kill any that survived the grenade. Rows of pillboxes stood between us and the top of the cliff. Slowly, one by one, we advanced forward. The bravery and gallantry of the soldiers was beyond belief. Soldiers were determined to do their job, regardless of the cost."

Excerpted from *Voices of D-Day: The Story of the Allied Invasion Told by Those Who Were There,* edited by Ronald J. Drez (Baton Rouge, LA, Louisiana State University Press, 1996). Copyright © 1996 by Louisiana State University Press. Reprinted with permission.

Road to Berlin

In early March 1945, the Allied armies in Western Europe crossed the Rhine River and entered Germany. The Nazi military machine was collapsing both in the east and the west. German soldiers surrendered in droves, especially to the British and American troops (because the Russians were believed to be brutal to their prisoners). There were still pockets of strong resistance, but often the Allied armies in the west would cover great distances in their advances into Germany.

Hal Boyle was a war correspondent who tagged along with a tank corps as it sped through the German countryside. Like the men he was with, Boyle believed he was heading straight for Berlin. But the American and British armies gave up that objective when they realized the Russians were also racing for the German capital. Still, the anticipation of victory over the Nazis was overpowering, and the Americans and British were jubilant as they covered more distance in a few days than they had in months of fighting in France.

This is the greatest armored joyride in history—and Adolf Hitler literally paved the way for his own downfall. The great single- and double-lane highways he built in peace to shuttle his armies out from the heart of Germany to attack neighboring countries are proving his undoing.

They are smooth concrete avenues to Berlin and other great German cities over which the mightiest masses of armor ever assembled in the west are now rolling at true blitzkrieg pace in a dozen columns, coming from so many directions the Germans are powerless to scrape together enough troops to halt them all.

The Nazi military machine has gone to pieces on its own home grounds. It is in chaos in many sectors. Tanks of Lt. Gen. Hodges's United States First Army and Lt. Gen. Patton's Third Army have yet to crack up against a really strong line—and there is none yet in sight.

Hodges has thrown into the grinding combat the largest tank task forces ever used by any American army on one battlefront—force which make El Alamein [a major battle in North Africa] look like a sandlot maneuver. And other attacking Allied armies have armored strength almost as powerful. . . .

Minefields, road blocks and antitank guns slow these giant columns only momentarily. Doughboys leap from the iron tanks and sweep in from the flanks to drive away or kill the enemy antitank gunners with rifle fire. Bulldozers move up in front of the column under cover of protecting tank guns and shove aside road-blocking debris from blown bridges and overhead spans as combat engineers sweep a path through the minefields. Then the column smashes forward again at full speed.

Whenever the columns run into a strong enemy position, one section coils off to deal with it as the rest of the tanks wheel onward. In this leapfrog fashion doughboy and tank teams have kept up the impetus of the advance.

They have swept through some towns so fast the householders hadn't time to put up white flags of surrender and the surprised Nazi garrisons were caught outside their positions, their guns unmanned. After a few minutes shelling they give up readily and infantry units then move in to clean out the snipers.

No attempt is being made to save Nazi real estate. Whenever the tankmen suspect a building or home may house a German strongpoint, they blow it apart and race by.

"When in doubt—fire first," is their motto.

Armored vehicles escort ammunition and food trains trailing behind the far-ranging columns and guard them from ambush. Despite advances of twenty to thirty-five miles a day, no tank has run out of shells and no man has gone without food.

Excerpted from "Road to Berlin: Hal Boyle Rides Along at Full Speed with Rampaging American Military Machine," by the Associated Press, March 27, 1945. Copyright © 1945 by the Associated Press. Reprinted with permission.

Liberating Buchenwald

As the Allied armies fought their way into Germany, they learned of the enemy's tenacity and fighting spirit. They had never guessed, however, at the depths of brutality and evil that lay at the heart of the Nazi cause. Some American soldiers were to come face to face with the horrors perpetrated by the Third Reich when they crossed the Elbe River in an effort to link with the Russian armies driving westward. In towns along this route, the GI's of the Twelfth Army discovered and liberated the concentration camps of Buchenwald, Dachau, and Bergen-Belsen. In these infernal prisons, millions of Jews, Slavs, gypsies, political prisoners, and other undesirables were put to death by Hitler's order. Little news of the concentration camps had ever reached America, and what horror stories did were often disbelieved as too fantastic. The American soldiers who came across these houses of the dead and dying were unprepared for what they saw.

Harry Herder was a nineteen-year-old private in April 1945 when his unit entered Buchenwald. The tanks in Herder's unit crashed through the gates of the camp and came to a halt in the main courtyard. Herder recalls how stunned he was by the sights and odors that greeted him.

I remember scouting out the area in front of us quickly with my eyes. There were no great details, but I saw that over to the left, next to, and just inside of the fence, and to our front, were some major buildings, and next to one of those buildings was a monster of a chimney, a monster both in diameter and in height. Black smoke was pouring out of it, and blowing away from us, but we could still smell it. An ugly horrible smell. A vicious smell. . . .

Slowly, as we formed up, a ragged group of human beings started to creep out of and from between the buildings in front

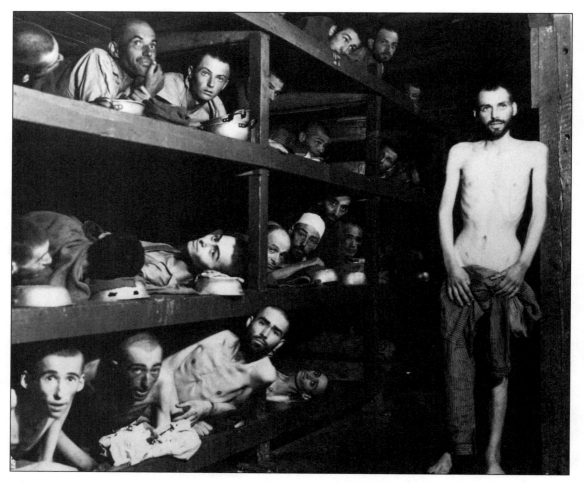

Prisoners at the Buchenwald concentration camp were liberated by American forces in April 1945.

of us. As we watched these men, the number and the different types of buildings came to my attention. From them came these human beings, timidly, slowly, deliberately showing their hands, all in a sort of uniform, or bits and pieces of a uniform, made from horribly coarse cloth with stripes running vertically. The stripes alternating a dull gray with a dark blue. Some of those human beings wore pants made of the material, some had shirt/jackets, and some had hats. Some only had one piece of the uniform, others had two, many had all three parts. They came out of the buildings and just stood there. . . .

The jeeps, our company commander's and a few others, rolled forward very slowly toward these people, and, as they parted, drove slowly through them, to the brick building next to that tall chimney, and our officers disappeared inside. Our platoon sergeant had us form up some and relax, then signaled that horde of human beings to stand fast; he just held both hands up, palms out, and motioned them backwards slowly. Everything was very quiet. The tanks were all in slow idle.

Hesitatingly we inched closer to that strange group as they also started inching closer to us. Some of them spoke English, and asked, "Are you American?" We said we were, and the reaction of the whole mass was immediate: simultaneously on their faces were relaxation, ease, joy, and they all began chattering to us in a babble of tongues that we couldn't answer. . . .

It was then that the smell of the place started to get to me. Our noses, rebelling against the surroundings they were constantly subjected to were not functioning anywhere near normally. But now there was a new odor, thick and hanging, and it assaulted the senses.

There was still space between us and the group in front of us, the people on both sides now relaxed, one side considerably more jubilant than the other, but all of the tensions were gone. We were inching closer together when our platoon sergeant was called back to one of the tanks and got on the radio. He wasn't there but a few minutes, came back, formed up our platoon, and took us back away, toward the place where we had entered the camp, back toward the fences through which we had

ripped holes. At each hole in the fence he left two of us. . . . We hadn't the vaguest idea what we had run into. Not yet. . . .

Containing the prisoners was not expected to be any trouble because they understood the need, and they were being provided for in every way that we could think of: the field hospital had just arrived, a big mess unit was on the way, loads of PX rations were coming. Sergeant Blowers told us that some of the prisoners spoke English. Then he got even quieter, looked at the ground for a moment, raised his eyes, and looking over our heads, began very softly, so softly we could barely hear him. He told us that this is what was called a "concentration camp", that we were about to see things we were in no way prepared for. He told us to look, to look as long as our stomachs lasted, and then to get out of there for a walk in the woods. . . .

Bill, Tim, and I started off through the trees, down the hill to the front gate which was only a couple of hundred yards away. The gate was a rectangular hole through the solid face of the building over which was office space and a hallway. High up above the opening for the gate was a heavy wooden beam with words carved into it in German script, Arbeit Macht Frei. In a clumsy way I attempted to translate the inscription to Bill and Tim as, "Work will make you free". The three of us headed through the gate, through the twenty or thirty feet to the other side of the building. We were slightly apprehensive of what we might see. . . . The lane we were walking on bent to the right as we cleared the building. We had barely made the turn, and there it was. In front of us a good bit, but plainly visible.

The bodies of human beings were stacked like cord wood. All of them dead. All of them stripped. The inspection I made of the pile was not very close, but the corpses seemed to be all male. The bottom layer of the bodies had a north/south orientation, the next layer went east/west, and

A deceptive sign reading "Work will make you free" hangs above the entrance at Buchenwald.

they continued alternating. The stack was about five feet high, maybe a little more; I could see over the top. They extended down the hill, only a slight hill, for fifty to seventy-five feet. Human bodies neatly stacked, naked, ready for disposal. The arms and legs were neatly arranged, but an occasional limb dangled oddly. The bodies we could see were all face up. There was an aisle, then another stack, and another aisle, and more stacks. The Lord only knows how many there were.

Just looking at these bodies made one believe they had been starved to death. They appeared to be skin covering bones and nothing more. The eyes on some were closed, on others open. Bill, Tim, and I grew very quiet. I think my only comment was, "Jesus Christ.". . .

The three of us looked, and we walked down the edge of those stacks. I know I didn't count them—it wouldn't have mattered. We looked and said not a word. A group of guys from the company noticed us and said, "Wait till you see in there."

They pointed to a long building which was about two stories high, and butted up tightly to the chimney. It had two barn-like doors on either end of the building we were looking at, and the doors were standing open. . . . We moved . . . through the doors and felt the warmth immediately. Not far from the doors, and parallel to the front of the building, there was a brick wall, solid to the top of the building. In the wall were small openings fitted with iron doors. Those doors were a little more than two feet wide and about two and a half feet high; the tops of the doors had curved shapes much like the entrances to churches. Those iron doors were in sets, three high. There must have been more than ten of those sets, extending down that brick wall. Most of the doors were closed, but down near the middle a few stood open. Heavy metal trays had been pulled out of those openings, and on those trays were partially burned bodies. On one tray was a skull partially burned through, with a hole in the top; other trays held partially disintegrated arms and legs. It appeared that those trays could hold three bodies at a time. And the odor, my God, the odor.

I had enough. I couldn't take it any more. I left the building with Bill and Tim close behind me. As we passed through the door someone from the company said, "the crematorium." Until then I had no idea what a crematorium was.

It dawned on me much later—the number of bodies which could be burned at one time, three bodies to a tray, at least thirty trays—and the Germans still couldn't keep up. The bodies on the stacks outside were growing at a faster rate than they could be burned. . . .

All of the German guards had packed up and moved out about three hours before our arrival. . . . When the Germans left, the crematorium was still going full blast, burning up a storm, the chimney belching out that black smoke. Our First Sergeant, Sergeant Blowers, our Company Commander, and the Leader of the TD group found

the source of the fuel, and played around with one thing and another until they figured out how to turn the damned thing off.

That was the start. That was just the "openers". There was more, but it was impossible to assimilate it all at once.

Excerpted from "Liberation of Buchenwald," by Harry Jerder Jr., *Liberators.* http://remember.org/witness/liberators.html.

Judgment at Nuremberg

Soon after war's end, the Allies organized an international military tribunal at Nuremberg, Germany to try captured Nazi officials and military leaders. Twenty-two top Nazis were judged, and of these, twelve were condemned to death for war crimes. One of the condemned, Air Minister Hermann Goering, committed suicide while in captivity, but the remaining Nazis went to the hangman's scaffold on October 16, 1946.

Kingsbury Smith, a reporter for the International News Service, witnessed the executions. He told of how most of the Nazis went to their deaths silently or with words bespeaking future peace in the world. Julius Streicher, a publisher of extremist anti-Semitic views, was an exception. Smith noted how when Streicher ascended the scaffold, he was antagonistic and remorseless.

Streicher appeared in the execution hall, which had been used only last Saturday night for a basketball game by American security guards, at twelve and a half minutes after two o'clock.

As in the case of all the condemned, a warning knock by a guard outside preceded

Nazi officials await their judgments at the Nuremberg trials.

Streicher's entry through a door in the middle of the hall.

An American lieutenant colonel sent to fetch the condemned from the death-row of the cell block to the near-by prison wing entered first. He was followed by Streicher, who was stopped immediately inside the door by two American sergeants. They closed in on each side of him and held his arms while another sergeant removed the manacles from his hands and replaced them with a leather cord.

The first person whom Streicher and the others saw upon entering the gruesome hall was an American lieutenant colonel who stood directly in front of him while his hands were being tied behind his back as they had been manacled upon his entrance.

This ugly, dwarfish little man, wearing a threadbare suit and a well-worn bluish shirt buttoned to the neck but without a tie, glanced at the three wooden scaffolds rising up menacingly in front of him.

Two of these were used alternately to execute the condemned men while the third was kept in reserve.

After a quick glance at the gallows, Streicher glared around the room, his eyes resting momentarily upon the small group of American, British, French, and Russian officers on hand to witness the executions.

By this time Streicher's hands were tied securely behind his back. Two guards, one to each arm, directed him to No. 1 gallows on the left entrance. He walked steadily the six feet to the first wooden step, but his face was twitching nervously. As the guards stopped him at the bottom of the steps for official identification requests, he uttered his piercing scream:

"Heil Hitler!"

His shriek sent a shiver down the back of this International News Service correspondent, who is witnessing the executions as sole representative of the American press.

As its echo died away, another American colonel standing by the steps said sharply:

"Ask the man his name."

In response to the interpreter's query Streicher shouted:

"You know my name well."

The interpreter repeated his request, and the condemned man yelled:

"Julius Streicher."

As he mounted the platform Streicher cried out:

"Now it goes to God!"

After getting up the thirteen steps to the eight-foot-high and eight-foot-square black-painted wooden platform, Streicher was pushed two steps to the mortal spot beneath the hangman's rope.

This was suspended from an iron ring attached to a crossbeam which rested on two posts. The rope was being held back against a wooden rail by the American Army sergeant hangman.

Streicher was swung around to face toward the front.

He glanced again at the Allied officers and the eight Allied correspondents representing the world's press who were lined up against a wall behind small tables directly facing the gallows.

With burning hatred in his eyes, Streicher looked down upon the witness and then screamed:

"Purim Fest 1946!"

The American officer standing at the scaffold said:

"Ask the man if he has any last words."

When the interpreter had translated, Streicher shouted:

"The Bolsheviks will hang you one day."

As the black hood was being adjusted about his head, Streicher was heard saying:

"Adele, my dear wife."

At that moment the trap was sprung with a loud bang. With the rope snapped taut and the body swinging wildly, a groan could be heard distinctly within the dark interior of the scaffold.

[Purim is a Jewish holiday celebrated in the spring and commemorating the hanging of Haman, Biblical oppressor of the Jews.]

Excerpted from "Ten Nazi Leaders Pay on the End of a Rope for Their Crimes," by Kingsbury Smith, *Journal-American,* October 16, 1946. Copyright © 1946 by United Press International. Reprinted with permission.

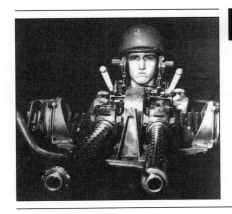

Chapter 4

War in the Pacific

When the Japanese initiated war with the United States in 1941, their goal was to secure as many vital South Pacific islands as possible. Because Japan was a nation of few resources, it needed to scavenge conquered lands to maintain its war effort. In the months following the attack on Pearl Harbor, Japanese forces seized Hong Kong, Malaya, and the Philippines. When America lost control of the Philippines it was as devastating as the crippling of the Pacific Fleet at Pearl Harbor. As a result General Douglas MacArthur's American and Filipino army, the main U.S. ground force in the Pacific, was forced to retreat. With no where to escape on the island nation, most of the army was eventually forced to surrender by April 1942. MacArthur, himself, was ordered by President Roosevelt to abandon his men and fly to safe harbor in Australia. From there, MacArthur vowed that he would head a new command that would retake the islands and revenge the humiliating American defeat.

Although the United States had the will to fight a ground war in the Pacific, it needed time to gather its strength. Until then, the Navy's aircraft carriers were given the task of stopping the Japanese. On May 7 and 8, as the Japanese sought to conquer New Guinea, an American carrier task force held them off in the costly battle of the Coral Sea. Although the Japanese were not successful, the American fleet lost one of its precious aircraft carriers.

However, in June, a second carrier battle proved to be the turning point of the Pacific war. The Japanese had planned to conquer the small island of Midway, a base that would give them command of much of the eastern Pacific. American intelligence intercepted the coded invasion instructions and laid a trap for the Japanese. In a pitched battle—with both sides sending planes to attack each other's carrier task forces—the Americans eventually gained the upper hand. Three Japanese carriers went down on the first day of battle; a fourth followed on the morning of the second day. The U.S. fleet lost one carrier, but the battle was a decisive American victory. With its limited resources, the Japanese could not replace its carriers. The United States, on the other hand, was adding to its navy nearly every month.

By the summer of 1942, the Japanese empire had reached its peak. Despite America's involvement in North Africa, the United States committed four-fifths of its men and material to the Pacific theater in that year. MacArthur was building his army rapidly in Australia when word came that the Japanese were constructing an airfield on Guadalcanal, a tiny island at the southern end of the Solomon Islands chain. The Solomons lay just east of New Guinea and a base there could threaten the air and naval lifeline between the United States and Australia.

In August 1942, the U.S. Marines staged an amphibious invasion of Guadalcanal. The Americans overtook the airfield and used it against the Japanese defenders on the is-

An American tank and infantrymen fight Japanese soldiers in New Guinea.

land. But, as the marines would learn in countless other island battles, the Japanese soldiers were experts at jungle warfare. The Japanese also did not typically surrender, meaning the Americans had to expend more effort to annihilate the enemy. As the Japanese fended off American attacks on Guadalcanal, they sent naval and air support to the Solomons. Each time, the Americans met them in terrific battles. Although the U.S. Navy and Air Force paid a high price, they held off each Japanese attempt to take the island. Worst of all for the Japanese, these missions sacrificed ships and planes that were not easily replaced. Yet, even with no support, the Japanese defenders on Guadalcanal fought on until February 1943.

In the summer of 1943, MacArthur finally had the forces he needed to begin his new conquest of the Pacific. Four American divisions and six Australian divisions moved up the Solomon Islands chain, securing some islands and leaving other, less important ones alone. This strategy became known as island hopping since the Allied armies would leapfrog up the Pacific island networks leaving Japanese forces isolated on the islands that were not directly invaded. Supported by naval carrier fleets and air force bombers taking off from makeshift airfields on captured islands, the Allied ground forces liberated much of the Solomon, Gilbert, and Marshall Islands chains by early 1944. Japan's navy had mostly been eradicated, and what remained was susceptible to the impressive array of

An American fighter plane returns to its carrier in the China Sea after an air attack near the Philippines.

nearly one hundred American carriers that now patrolled the Pacific.

In June, as Allied armies went ashore in Normandy, France, American marines hit the beaches of Saipan, a small island in the Marianas. After a bloody fight, the marines cleared the Marianas Islands and gained air bases from which to launch long-range bombers against Japan itself. By October, the air force was not only pounding Japanese cities but was also softening up defenses in the Philippines. In that month, MacArthur began to make good on his promise to retake those islands by landing on the southern island of Leyte. Incensed, the Japanese navy attempted to strike back against the invasion fleet. But American naval power—and more importantly air power—could not be overcome. With so few warplanes of its own left, the air arm of the Japanese fleet was eliminated in the ensuing battle. Furthermore, this left the unguarded Japanese ships easy prey for American bombers.

As marines fought to liberate Leyte, MacArthur continued his island hopping tactics by sending other forces against other islands in the Philippines. On March 4, 1945 the capital of Manila was freed, and a good part of its large home island was secured. The Japanese had lost four hundred and fifty thousand men in the struggle for the Philippines, and now there was little between the Americans and the Japanese home islands. In fact while the battle for Manila was still going on, MacArthur had already sent forces against a small island just

General Douglas MacArthur goes ashore during the initial landing at Leyte.

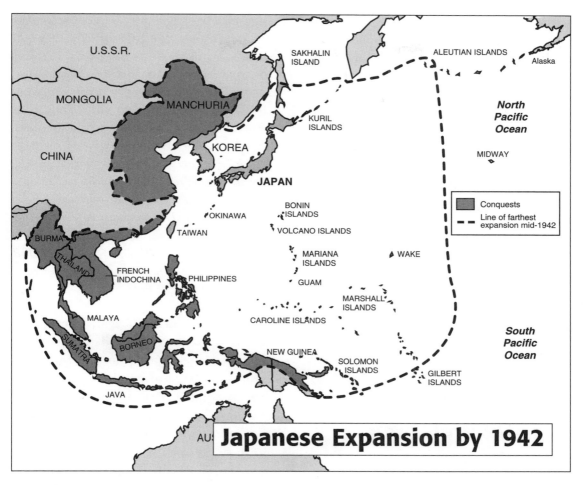

Japanese Expansion by 1942

south of the Japanese island of Honshu. On Iwo Jima, a volcanic rock, the Americans would face some of the stiffest resistance yet in the Pacific war. Iwo Jima was not terribly important, but its neighbor, Okinawa, was. Okinawa had a good harbor and could serve as an excellent staging point for an invasion of the Japanese mainland only three hundred and fifty miles away.

The invasion of Okinawa began in April. The Japanese air force had more than one hundred thousand men and three thousand aircraft on the island, all of which were sacrificed in its defense. When Okinawa fell, Japan lay open to invasion.

All through March and early April, American bombers had devastated Japan's cities. Tokyo, Kobe, Osaka—all were destroyed by explosions and resulting fires. Still, the Japanese government did not give in. Recognizing that the Japanese would make any invasion force pay dearly for each yard of Japanese soil conquered, President Harry S. Truman—who took over after Roosevelt's untimely death—decided upon another plan. A new atomic weapon had been developed, and Truman hoped that by utilizing it, the costly invasion of Japan could be avoided. On August 6, 1945, the Americans dropped its first atomic bomb on Hiroshima. The devastation was amazing. Yet, only after a second bomb was dropped on Nagasaki on August 9 did Japan sue for peace. After the years of struggle, the denouement to the Pacific war was completed in a matter of days. Although the world returned to a state of peace, the horrific new weapons used to end the war would come to symbolize fear that another much more deadly war could occur in the future.

The Bataan Death March

Soon after the surprise attack at Pearl Harbor, Japanese ground forces invaded the Philippines. U.S. and Filipino forces fought a losing battle on the main island of Luzon, and the survivors were pushed onto the Bataan peninsula and the island of Corregidor. For ten weeks, the defenders of these two tiny pieces of land held off repeated Japanese assaults. Eventually, low on food and ammunition, the U.S. and Filipino soldiers were forced to surrender on April 10, 1942.

The survivors of Bataan were marched fifty-five miles to a railhead where they were then dispersed to prison camps. Along the way, the

Americans and Filipinos were subjected to inhuman cruelty from their captors. Of the 76,000 men who began the Death March, 2,330 Americans and between 7 and 10,000 Filipinos died en route. News of the tragedy, however, did not immediately reach the outside world. Only when the army and navy posted an official report in 1944 did the horrors come to light.

Air force Captain (later Colonel) William E. Dyess was one of the lucky ones who made it to a prison camp. He then escaped after spending a year in captivity. His testimony concerning the Bataan march was included in the War Department's report. Tragically, Dyess was later killed in a plane crash as he was preparing to return to the fight in the Pacific.

"The march of death" began when thousands of prisoners were herded together at Mariveles airfield on Bataan at daylight on April 10, 1942, after their surrender. Though some had food, neither Americans nor Filipinos were permitted by their guards to eat any of it. They were searched and their personal belongings taken from them. Those who had Japanese tokens or money in their possession were beheaded.

In groups of 500 to 1,000 men, the prisoners were marched along the national road of Bataan toward San Fernando, in Pampanga province. Those marchers who still had personal belongings were stripped of them; the Japanese slapped and beat them with sticks, as they marched along without food or water on a scorchingly hot day. Colonel Dyess, in a middle group, gave this description of "the march of death":

"A Japanese soldier took my canteen, gave the water to a horse, and threw the canteen away. We passed a Filipino prisoner of war who had been bayoneted. Men recently killed were lying along the roadside, many had been run over and flattened by Japanese trucks.

"Many American prisoners were forced to act as porters for military equipment. Such treatment caused the death of a sergeant in my squadron, the 31st Pursuit. Patients bombed out of a near-by hospital, half dazed and wandering about in pajamas and slippers, were thrown into our marching column of prisoners. What their fate was I do not know. At 10 o'clock that night we were forced to retrace our march of two hours, for no apparent reason.

"At midnight we were crowded into an enclosure too narrow to lie down. An officer asked permission to get water and a Japanese guard beat him with a rifle butt. Finally a Japanese officer permitted us to drink water from a near-by carabao wallow.

"Before daylight the next morning, the 11th, we were awakened and marched down the road. Japanese trucks speeded by. A Japanese soldier swung his rifle from one of them in passing, and knocked any American prisoner unconscious beside the road.

"Through the dust clouds and blistering heat, we marched that entire day without food. We were allowed to drink dirty water from a roadside stream at noon. Some time later three officers were taken from our marching column, thrown into an automobile and driven off. I never learned what became of them. They never arrived at any of the prison camps.

"Our guards repeatedly promised us food, but never produced it. The night of the 11th, we again were searched and then the march resumed. Totally done in, American and Filipino prisoners fell out frequently, and threw themselves moaning beside the roadside. The stronger were not permitted to help the weaker. We then would hear shots behind us.

"At 3 o'clock on the morning of April 12 they shoved us into a barbed-wire bull pen big enough to accommodate 200. We were 1,200 inside the pen—no room to lie down; human filth and maggots were everywhere.

"Throughout the 12th, we were introduced to a form of torture which came to be known as the sun treatment. We were made to sit in the boiling sun all day long without cover. We had very little water; our thirst was intense. Many of us went crazy and several died. The Japanese dragged out the sick and delirious. Three Filipino and three American soldiers were buried while still alive.

"On the 13th, each of those who survived was given a mess kit of rice. We were given another full day of the sun treatment. At nightfall we were forced to resume our march. We marched without water until dawn of April 14, with one two-hour interval, when we were permitted to sit beside the roadside.

"The very pace of our march itself was a torture. Sometimes we had to go very fast, with the Japanese pacing us on bicycles. At other times, we were forced to shuffle along very slowly. The muscles of my legs began to draw and each step was an agony.

"Filipino civilians tried to help both Filipino and American soldiers by tossing us food and cigarettes from windows or from behind houses. Those who were caught were beaten. The Japanese had food stores along the roadside.

"A United States Army colonel pointed to some of the cans of salmon and asked for food for his men. A Japanese officer picked up a can and hit the colonel in the face with it, cutting his cheek wide open. Another colonel and a brave Filipino picked up three American soldiers before the Japs could get to them. They placed them on a cart and started down the road toward San Fernando. The Japanese seized them as well as the soldiers, who were in a coma, and horse-whipped them fiercely.

"Along the road in the province of Pampanga there are many wells. Half-crazed with thirst, six Filipino soldiers made a dash for one of the wells. All six were killed. As we passed Lubao we marched by a Filipino soldier gutted and hanging over a barbed-wire fence. Late that night of the 14th we were jammed into another bull pen at San Fernando with again no room to lie down. During the night Japanese soldiers with fixed bayonets charged into the compound to terrorize the prisoners.

"Before daylight on April 15 we were marched out and 115 of us were packed into a small narrow-gauge box car. The doors were closed and locked. Movement was impossible. Many of the prisoners were suffering from diarrhea and dysentery. The heat and stench were unbearable. We all wondered if we would get out of the box car alive.

"At Capiz Tarlac we were taken out and given the sun treatment for three hours. Then we were marched to Camp O'Donnell, a prison camp under construction, surrounded with barbed wire and high towers, with separate inner compounds of wire. On this last leg of the journey the Japanese permitted the stronger to carry the weaker.

"I made that march of about 85 miles in six days on one mess kit of rice. Other Americans made 'the march of death' in 12 days, without any food whatever. Much of the time, of course, they were given the sun treatment along the way."

Excerpted from "Joint Release by the U.S. Army and Navy," Washington, January 27, 1944.

Japanese Guts at Guadalcanal

In the summer of 1942, American armies in the Pacific were on the move, reclaiming land that the Japanese conquered in their initial military sweep following victory at Pearl Harbor. In the Solomon Islands, the target was Guadalcanal, an island known mainly for its airstrip. For months, Japanese planes from Guadalcanal had harassed shipping lanes to Australia. The U.S. command in the Pacific decided to invade the tiny island, seize the airstrip, and use it to the Allies' advantage.

On August 7, 1942, U.S. Marines landed at Guadalcanal and neighboring islands. The marines seized the airstrip immediately, but the Japanese defenders on the island were far from beaten. They held the high ground around the small American beachhead. Fighting was vicious as the marines held off numerous counterattacks. It took four months to quell the Japanese opposition at a cost of thousands of American lives.

Ira Wolfert, a Pulitzer Prize winning correspondent for the North American Newspaper Alliance, was on Guadalcanal in November 1943. He wrote of the zealous do-or-die mentality of the Japanese defenders that held up the American progress on Guadalcanal and countless other islands in the Pacific.

In the five battles of the Solomons, the least we have done is keep the Japs from winning—which is victory, in a military sense when a long, hard war is still in its preliminary stages—and in our biggest successes, in the fourth and fifth battles, we not only have kept the Japs from winning, but have made them pay heavily for trying to win.

We've licked the Japs on land, on sea, and in the air. We've shown that we have more military brains than they have, are better at war, all kinds of war, from strangling and knife-fighting and head-trampling on up into the complicated mechanized operations of modern battle. The Solomons haven't shown yet that we can outproduce the Japs, but we think that's true, that we can make as good material as anybody and can make more of it than the Japs, and can replace it faster than they can.

But there's one thing that nobody in the world can be better at than the Japs and that's in the guts department. They have more guts than the Germans have. At least, they have shown thus far in the Solomons deal, which is the first deal where they've had to hold their chins out and take it, that they have more guts. The Germans have said "Kamerad" [I surrender] in the past and may be relied on to say it in the future. But the Japs have never surrendered, never *en masse*, and only rarely as individuals. We have not yet taken a single officer alive on Guadalcanal, although we have tried in every way we know how. And the great majority of the few soldier prisoners we have taken have been wounded and in a condition where their minds have not been up to par.

Every day I was there, the Jap gave new evidence of his intense willingness to go to any lengths to win, or, if unable to win, to go on fighting until his breath stopped. . . .

Under the heading of willingness to go on fighting, this story may be told. I haven't my notes with me, and I can't remember this Marine captain's name, but everybody called him Wimpy. Wimpy was out on patrol and ran into some Japs holed up in a native hut. Quite a hot little brush followed, and after about fifteen minutes our side got no more answering fire.

Wimpy crawled up close and saw that all the Japs were dead except one, who seemed badly wounded. This one was lying on the floor of the hut in a corner farthest from the door. He was bleeding from the mouth and stared solemnly at Wimpy, and Wimpy decided to try taking him prisoner.

For twenty minutes, Wimpy cajoled and begged and tried everything he knew, waving a handkerchief as a flag of truce, offering "pogie bait," as the Marines call candy, as a bribe. The Jap did not answer. The blood flowed steadily from his mouth and his face occasionally broke under pain, but he just stared solemnly at Wimpy.

So the Marine captain decided to go in after the man. He went in the door, holding his revolver in his hand, and stood there pointing the revolver. He stood as far away as he could because wounded Japs, so hurt they could not throw a grenade, have been known to pull the pin as somebody comes near them and blow up the reckless one as well as themselves.

So Wimpy stayed as far away as possible and pointed his gun. The Jap lifted himself to his hands and knees and began to crawl toward a dead Jap officer who was wearing a sword. "Don't do that!" cried Wimpy, "I'll have to shoot you." Wimpy didn't dare go near the man. All he could do was point his gun and shout. The Jap kept crawling slowly for the sword and took out the sword and Wimpy stamped his foot and shouted, "You damn fool! Oh, you damn damn fool! I'll have to kill you." Then the Jap lifted himself to his feet and lifted the sword over his head and started for Wimpy, and Wimpy had to shoot him dead.

These are not exceptional cases. They are typical. So there can be no question of our being better fighters than the Japs. The best anybody can possibly do is be as good, and rely on our superiority in all other de-partments of war to give us the victory in the long run.

PT Boat Squadron

During the battles in the Solomon Islands, many newsmen reported on the land war on Guadalcanal and neighboring Tulagi, but few addressed the naval conflict that raged in the waters around these islands. John Hersey was a war correspondent in 1942 when he covered events in the South Pacific for the Time *news syndicate. Hersey was entranced by the bravery of the unsung sailors in the Solomons. One of the units that interested him was PT Squadron X, a small fleet of torpedo boats that carried on hit and run actions against the Japanese navy in the region. The squadron caught his attention because the stories that its officers told were not of single heroes staging remarkable feats, but rather of a disciplined unit acting together to pull off the impossible. For this reason, Hersey decided to tell the tale of PT Squadron X in the first person plural.*

"Everyone has heard of the great battle of Guadalcanal, November 12 to 15, when we broke the Japs' backs. The squadron had been in action almost continuously for ten days and we knew the Japs were making their big attempt. Everybody was very tired and had the shakes. On the night of the 13th-14th, there were only five boats left in condition to patrol and one patrol had already been out, so that left only three boats running. But a big Japanese battleship had been reported hanging around all day with lots of destroyers, so we took our three saucy rigs out against it.

"First we had to screen one of our crippled ships that was being towed in. Then they sent us over for the big game. The Japs were shelling Henderson Field [on Guadalcanal]. They had put a flare up which lit up things nicely for us. One ship appeared heavier than the others; either a battleship or a heavy cruiser. Stilly got on a collision course, approached to 1,200 yards, fired a spread and moved away without ever having been seen. At least one torpedo found its target. Then Jack fired and got two hits

on one of the screening destroyers. Our best results came from what seemed to be the easiest attacks like this one.

"We fired 18 torpedoes that night. Every time we fired a spread, we used to think, 'Golly, there go 40,000 bucks.' This night we spent $180,000. But we figure we cost the Japs plenty more than that.

"When we came back in, there wasn't a fish [torpedo] left in any one of the tubes. Assembling and mounting torpedoes is a mean job. The way that job was handled the

PT marksman (left). A boat patrols in the Solomon Islands showed unusual courage against mounting odds.

A torpedoed Japanese destroyer seen through a periscope.

whole campaign. At the port director's office we were told that a Jap invasion fleet—not just a task force—was on its way. They also said: 'We may have a battleship task force, Admiral Lee's outfit, coming up here to meet the Japs but we're not sure. We want you fellows to sift through the destroyers and cruisers and get the transports.'

"It was certain suicide. Nik, for one, was dripping with sweat when he left that office. He didn't expect to live through the night. When he went aboard, his crew asked for the dope. He didn't have the heart to tell them. He said: 'I don't know for sure, I think some Japs are supposed to be coming down.'

"We got out on patrol and ran up and down like frightened terriers. Finally Robbie picked up the Japs. His radioman came up with a full voice and said: 'Here they are.' Robbie came on, just as dull, with 'Well, let's see what we can do.'

"We turned and there, just west of Savo Island, we saw them. Counting the mirages our frightened minds conjured, there were a thousand ships spread out. It was the greatest show of force any of us had ever imagined, much less seen. Even our boats seemed to tremble as we deployed for what we knew would be our last runs.

next day, so that three boats could go out with fish in them that night, was certainly a tribute to the base force. They went to work before the sky turned gray in the morning and they didn't knock off until it was too dark to see a thing. Then three boats were ready.

"No torpedoes were fired that night (November 14–15), but for those who were out it was the most terrific night of the

"Just then a cheery singsong voice, not one of us, came up on the radio. 'Boys, this is Ching Chong China Lee. So you know who I am?' We all knew that Admiral Lee had spent several years on the China station. Robbie's voice boomed out on the radio: 'Yes *sir*, we sure do!' He came back with: 'Get the hell out of the way. I'm coming through.'

"You have never seen three PT boats move the way we did. We almost took on altitude.

"We withdrew northward and saw Lee go by with his force. It was pathetically small, compared with what we had seen of the Japs, but it looked like mama to us little babies. We stopped our engines, went up on the foredeck, and half an hour later we were all sitting there eating sandwiches, sipping coffee and watching from a front-row seat one of the greatest battles of this war. It was just like sitting at Ebbets Field. Only different.

"We sat there for a time and nothing happened. Then somebody dropped flares. The destroyers opened fire first with some small stuff, over near Savo Island. A few ships exploded. Each explosion gave off some daylight. First we'd see a ship explode, then there'd be huge burning for a minute or so; then there would be another explosion, then there would be the burning again.

"Then the battleships began. There would be a little flash. Three red balls would then go into the sky, up, and over, and down, and then whoomp! A ship would blow up. We can't remember a single time those three red American balls went across

the sky without something being hit. It was unbelievable.

"The two groups of ships were operating about five miles apart. You could just sit there and watch this whole Jap fleet blowing up all night. The Japs fired too, with everything they had, but they just weren't as good. A couple of our destroyers did blow up. But the main impression was watching the three red balls.

"This went on for about an hour, or maybe two or three. It really didn't take very long to clean up that Japanese fleet. We were just sitting there the whole time, so impressed and amazed that nobody spoke for many minutes after the thing died down. Finally one of the men said: 'Jesus Christ, what a sight, what a sight!'

Excerpted from *History in the Writing*, edited by Gordon Carroll (New York, NY: Duell, Sloan & Pearce, 1945). Copyright © 1945 by Time, Inc. Reprinted with permission.

A Nurse in the South Pacific

The bravery of medical units that operated in World War II—as in many wars—was often overshadowed by the feats of the soldiers who fought in combat. Although not on the front lines, many doctors, nurses, and field hospital staff members performed their duties in less-than-ideal conditions, sometimes even within the range of enemy fire. Margaret Richey Raffa was an air force nurse who was sent to the South Pacific in 1943. In an interview later in life, she recalls what trials she and the other medical personnel faced on a daily basis while helping save the lives of wounded servicemen.

We were the first flight nurse squadron to go to the Pacific, landing in New Caledonia in February 1943. We enjoyed the temperature and flowers, which are equally beautiful there all year, but conditions were very primitive. The river behind our tents was our washing machine, and we hung clothes to dry from trees. There were twenty-four nurses, and millions of mosquitoes, all living in one tent. One night during the first week, the tent blew down during a typhoon, and our foot lockers almost floated away.

C-47s [acting as medical evacuation planes] flew to the front with cargo and ammunition, and the nurses rode on top of the cargo. We often had troops going to the forward areas, which was sad for us. They would get into long discussions, feeling that they would probably never come back. The worst part is, some of them didn't.

When we went to Guadalcanal, the plane wouldn't fly directly over the island but flew along the beach, staying low to avoid being spotted by the Japanese. This was emotionally trying for us, not knowing

A nurse stationed in the Philippines monitors a wounded American soldier.

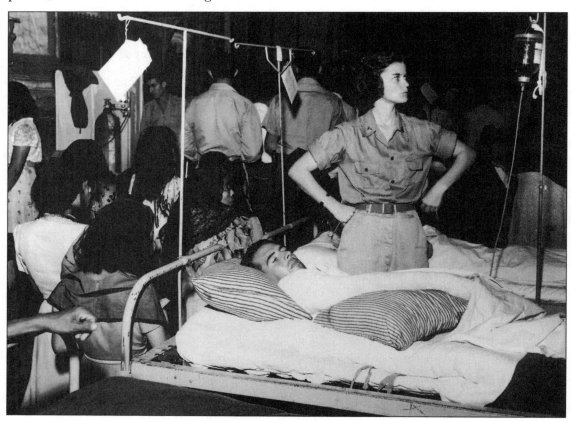

what the landing field would be like. There were no ambulances. The most seriously wounded patients would be on litters, with other wounded in different vehicles. We took off quickly because the Japanese were strafing [firing at] the field. Our casualties were still in rather bad shape, having had only first aid treatment. They had shrapnel and bullet wounds and injuries from hand grenades, often of the chest, abdomen, or head. It presented quite a problem, since there were no doctors on board, and we had to rely on our own initiative. We always had to be alert for symptoms of shock and hemorrhage, and from the time we took off until we landed, we had our hands full with these mutilated bodies. One nurse might have twenty-four patients, most of them on litters, for a five hour flight, and in those days we didn't have the [help of] enlisted medical technicians. We felt a tremendous responsibility.

Some patients were taken to the hospital in New Hebrides [Group of islands in the Southwest in the Pacific Ocean] and later evacuated back to the States, but there were general hospitals in New Caledonia where these patients received good enough care to be returned to duty. We took boys back up to the front lines a month or two after we'd brought them out wounded.

The problems were constant. For instance, after we reached [an altitude of] 8,000 feet there was a lack of oxygen, and often we climbed to 10,000 feet because of weather conditions. Then we had to give oxygen to patients continuously. Small oxygen tanks were all we had room for, and patients shared them. We did use alcohol on the tanks between patients, but it wasn't very sanitary. A lot of the planes didn't have heaters, and at 10,000 feet, even in the South Pacific, it was cold.

Sometimes we had to make forced landings because of maintenance or weather or fuel shortages, and this caused big problems for the commanding officers of the airstrips where we landed. Most of the time these fields were under attack by the Japanese, and we'd often have to head for foxholes [pits that provide cover from enemy fire], with the war being fought right above us. One time I was going to stand at the edge of a foxhole to watch as they went after a Japanese plane. A GI decided to head for the same place and hit my feet, knocking me over. I decided to stay down after that.

Excerpted from *No Time for Fear: Voices of the American Military Nurses in World War II*, by Diane Burke Fessler (East Lansing, MI: Michigan State University Press, 1996). Copyright © 1996 by Michigan State University Press. Reprinted with permission.

The Graves at Attu

Alaska's Aleutian Island chain stretches far into the Pacific Ocean. In 1942, the Japanese seized islands at the end of the chain, some one thousand miles from the Alaskan mainland. Their goal was to draw the American fleet away from Midway Island. Unwilling to give up American soil, the United States began an invasion of the occupied islands in late fall of that year. The retaking of the islands took some time. It was not until May 1943 that the Americans landed on Attu, a small island west of Kiska, the main Japanese base in the Aleutians.

Japanese naval aviators on Attu pose for a photographer.

Attu, like other volcanic islands in the chain, is almost always fogged in. The fighting there was conducted in freezing winds and cold mists. The Japanese defenders had burrowed into the earth and had to be routed out of their foxholes one by one. With defeat imminent, the Japanese command ordered a suicide charge in the hopes that they would inflict severe damage on the Americans while sacrificing their own lives. Of the 2,600 man garrison at Attu, the Americans captured only 28 prisoners. Though the Japanese suffered terrible losses, many Americans also died during the assault. War correspondent Robert Sherrod was on Attu when the mists cleared from the battlefield. He wrote an assessment of the carnage that he witnessed, and the manner in which the military took care of its dead.

The caterpillar tractors towed their trailers over the valleys and plateaus between Attu's high peaks all night. Today 125 of our dead are lined up for burial in the Little Falls Cemetery near Massacre Bay—one of our two graveyards on Attu. Mostly they are the results of the Jap's mad fanatical rush of Saturday and Sunday. Many are horribly mangled by bayonets and rifle butts. Many were obviously shot and killed, then stabbed time after time by the strange little yellow men who then proceeded to die, sometimes by their own hands, as violently as possible.

There will be more dead brought to the cemetery named for a nearby waterfall. It will take several days to collect all the Americans who made the supreme sacrifice on the precipitous slopes of this gray little island. Fortunately, the 40-degree weather does not require that we bury the dead immediately. After we have finished burying our own dead we will collect the enemy bodies and bury them.

No nation handles its casualties as carefully as we do. The 125 who lie in rows are examined meticulously. A medical officer records the cause of death and the number and type of wounds as each body is stripped. Members of the graves registration company cut open each pocket and recover the personal effects of the dead soldier, placing them in a clean wool sock for dispatch to the Quartermaster Depot at Kansas City. One identification tag is left on the body, the other is nailed to the cross which will be placed above the grave until a larger metal plate can be stamped. Graves are laid out in perfect geometrical pattern, then charted so that no mistake can be made in locating any body.

Three sets of fingerprints are made from the hands of each dead man. One set stays with the man's military unit, two are sent to the Adjutant General in Washington. (If a soldier's "dog tags" are missing and his personal effects carry no absolute identification, his body is not buried until some men from his unit have made positive identification.) After fingerprinting, the bodies are carried through the identification tent and wrapped in khaki blankets which are tied at three spots: around the neck, waist and feet. Bodies are laid in rows of eight, awaiting burial.

Graves are dug by bulldozers—there is not time nor labor to dig with shovels. The huge bulldozers plow back and forth until a space seven feet deep has been scooped out, which is long enough to place eight bodies 18 inches apart. Then in the collective grave, small one-foot-deep individual graves are dug by shovel. Thus, each man has his own grave beside seven of his comrades.

After the bodies are placed eight to the grave, a simple, dignified funeral service, lasting perhaps ten minutes, is said. Wherever possible Protestants are buried together, as are Catholics. It is legend on Attu that the chaplains have been as splendid under fire as any combat soldiers. Burying the dead is only a small part of the chaplain's work, but nothing concerns them more than that each body shall have services said over it.

Picture three chaplains standing over the bodies of eight khaki-blanketed bodies. The bulldozers, which are digging other graves, stop and their drivers uncover while the brief services are continued, but the dozen of tractors on the muddy roads and beaches a few hundred yards away continue their clanking. The chaplains begin by singing the first verse, then the third verse of *Rock of Ages*. The graveside is dedicated by extemporaneous prayer when the services are ended; from 50 yards away two bugles play taps. The chaplains cover their heads and the graveyard bulldozer huff-puffs again, pushing mounds of cold Attu earth over the khaki-clad bodies of eight U.S. soldiers.

Denominational distinction is held to a minimum on Attu. The thirteen chaplains have assembled a joint prayer book. Whenever a Catholic chaplain is not available, a

Protestant may administer last rites to a dying soldier. Likewise, the Catholic burial service may be said by a Baptist chaplain or vice versa. Usually, as was the case this morning, the Catholic chaplain blesses the graves of Catholic soldiers whenever he returns.

There is no Jewish chaplain on Attu. Until today only four Jewish soldiers had been killed. Hebrew services were held for them by a medical officer, Capt. Jacob Fine of Milwaukee. He read the Jewish burial service from the abridged prayer book for Jews in the armed services, including the 23rd Psalm and the Kaddish, and the Memorial Prayer for those who have died in battle. Captain Fine, a popular little man who has grown a thick brown beard, makes a fine chaplain except for one thing: carried away by emotion, he cries like a baby.

Since the sudden influx of bodies following the fantastic Jap charge of last weekend, it has been necessary to augment the graves registration company with recruits. These men were not undertakers. They were clerks and truck drivers and farmers. Their reactions are sober. There is no excitement at this scene of wholesale death. Exception: one little soldier of Mexican descent, whose brother-in-law was killed in the early fighting, works about 18 hours a day burying the dead (everybody on Attu works about 18 hours a day). Then he takes a gun, slips away into the hills and hunts Jap snipers the rest of the night.

One young lieutenant from Mississippi, not long out of Officer Candidate School,

probably expressed everybody's feelings when he came upon the 125 bodies. Said he: "I wonder if those sons of bitches holding up war production back home wouldn't change their minds if they could look at this."

And They Call This Practice

James J. Fahey was a Seaman First Class aboard the cruiser USS Montpelier *during World War II. While serving his tour of duty in the Pacific, Fahey took part in many actions—from naval firefights to shore bombardments—against the Japanese. He wrote of his experiences in his book* Pacific War Diary.

Fahey's observations are acute and often tinged with the ironies of war. For example, in 1944, while operating off the island of Bougainville (in the Solomon chain) the Montpelier *was ordered to participate in gunnery practice against Japanese installations on the island. However, the targets were active Japanese pillboxes with large-caliber gun emplacements. As the* Montpelier *and other ships moved in to bombard the enemy positions, they came under the fire of the Japanese shore guns. To Fahey, the deadly exchange gave a whole new, uncomfortable meaning to the word "practice."*

Saturday, May 20, 1944: Arose at 4:30 A.M. We left Munda at 5:50 A.M. We will travel to Bougainville for more gunnery exercises against pillboxes. On the way to our destination, Captain Hoffman spoke to the crew, saying that our targets will be live. There are still Japs on the end of the island that we will be shooting at. Shore batteries are reported there by a destroyer that was passing when the guns opened up on it. The Captain believed that the Japs there were being supplied by enemy submarines. This will be only classified as a practice run but return fire by the Japs is anticipated. We got quite a kick out of the Captain's phraseology. Having six inch shells being fired at us by the enemy, and they rate it practice. Planes will spot for us, informing us of our accuracy. We will have four destroyers and the cruisers *Cleveland* and *Birmingham* with us.

Arriving at 10 A.M., we commenced firing at 10:35 A.M. The Jap shore batteries on the beach returned the fire quickly after. Their guns were stationed on top of a hill. Their guns that were firing at us were the big 8 inch variety. Our largest caliber was the 6 inch. Our run on Bougainville was commencing as our starboard guns opened fire. On returning the port guns were brought into action. The first ship to be fired at by the enemy shore batteries, was the cruiser *Cleveland*. I was at my battle station on the 40 mm. machine gun mount and the Admiral and Captain were just above me on the bridge. As I looked to the rear, I saw big geysers of water, rising all around the cruiser *Cleveland*. It was a miracle that it was not hit. At first we took it as a joke, but then got very serious because we knew that our turn would come to be fired

on by the big Jap guns. Cruisers make a very big target in the daytime, they are over six hundred feet long. While we were on our way in to hit the Japs, they opened up on us. They must have had us in their sights, because their big 8 inch shells began to explode all around us and fly through the mast, they could not have come any closer without hitting us. In the meantime our guns were blazing away but the Japs were in a very difficult spot for us to hit, behind a hill. We could not get any closer to the Japs, because it would be suicide. We could see the big flashes from their guns as they kept up a steady fire with their 8 inch guns against our six inch guns. The Jap shells sent big sprays of water up into the air just in front of my mount and one of the 20 mm. gun mounts up forward on the bow was knocked out by shrapnel, as it sprayed the ship with big chunks of red hot steel. Some of the wounded were carried to the crew's lounge, it is a battle dressing station. One Marine named Darling had a big piece of shrapnel go through his helmet and out the other side. When they picked up his helmet part of his scalp was still in it. One fellow almost went insane with the pain, and he was going to jump over the side. . . .

If our ship was going a little faster the Admiral and Captain would have got it and we are very close to them. You hold your breath when you see the Jap guns fire at you and then wait to see if they hit you. They could not come any closer without hitting us. It does not feel very good to see 8 inch shells falling all around you and you have no place to hide. One of the fellows dove for the deck when he heard the shells close by explode and an officer dove on top of him, we got a kick out of it. A piece of shrapnel about six by six almost hit Gallagher, and he had to pick it up with his hat because it was so hot. When shrapnel hits thick steel it bounces around. The anchor chain which is about as thick as a football was almost cut in half. Someone said the *Cleveland* also got hit. If the Japs ever hit us with direct hits, they would have done an awful lot of damage and you do not know what it might have led to, it could have sunk us. The Japs didn't interfere with our . . . "practice," because we stayed here for two hours firing at them.

Our ship knocked out the Jap radio tower and some anti-aircraft guns, we also helped knock out some of the big shore batteries. The cruiser *Cleveland* fired over a thousand rounds of six inch shells not to mention what the rest of us fired. The Japs must have thought they were at a shooting gallery firing these big 8 inch guns at us and shell and shrapnel falling all around us. Those Japs have plenty of guts, they are not afraid of anything. This was a good old fashion slugfest, with no quarter given by either side. No one was brokenhearted when we finally left, and they call this practice. What will the new men who just come from the States think. They will hate to face the real McCoy.

Excerpted from *Pacific War Diary: 1942–1945,* by James J. Fahey, (Boston, MA: Houghton Mifflin, 1963). Copyright © 1963 by James J. Fahey. Reprinted with permission.

The Turkey Shoot

In June, 1944, only a few days after the invasion of Normandy in Europe, Admiral Chester Nimitz's naval fleet attacked Saipan in the Marianas Islands. The Pacific war had been a seesaw battle up until then, but Japan had incurred some losses that the small nation could not recoup. In the air war, Japan had lost hard-to-replace aircraft and, more significantly, impossible-to-replace expert pilots. The Americans had also finally produced fighter planes that could match and even outperform the deadly Japanese Zero.

The aircraft carriers in Nimitz's invasion fleet were given the task of keeping the skies clear over Saipan. Japanese fighter, bomber, and torpedo planes, however, contested American superiority. But the shortcomings of the Japanese planes and the lack of sufficient fighter protection gave the advantage to the American pilots. Relatively defenseless Japanese bombers and torpedo planes were swamped by the American fighters in what came to be called the Great Marianas Turkey Shoot.

Alex Vraciu was a Hellcat pilot on the aircraft carrier USS Lexington. In one eight-minute period during the Turkey Shoot, Vraciu shot down six planes, unbelievably becoming an ace in one day. In an interview with Irv Broughton decades later, Vraciu recalled the moments after he was notified enemy planes were heading toward his squadron as it flew just above the American fleet. After racking up nineteen more air victories in other combats, Vraciu became the top navy ace, a title he would hold for four months in 1944.

Spot-gazing intently, I suddenly picked out a large, rambling mass of at least 50 enemy planes 2,000 feet below us, port side and closing. My adrenaline flow was high. The Japanese were about 35 miles from our forces and heading in fast. I remember thinking that this could develop into that once-in-a-lifetime fighter pilot's dream. Puzzled and suspicious, I looked about for the fighter cover that one would expect over their attacking planes, but none was seen. By this time we were in perfect position for a high side run on the enemy aircraft. I rocked my wings and began a run on the nearest inboard straggler, a Judy dive-bomber. Peripherally I was conscious of another Hellcat having designs on that Jap also. He was too close for comfort and seemed not to see me, so I aborted my run. There were enough cookies on this plate for everyone, I was thinking. Streaking underneath the formation, I had a good look at the enemy planes for the first time. They were Judys [bombers], Jills [torpedo bombers] and Zeroes [fighters]. I radioed an amplified report.

After pulling up and over, I picked up another Judy on the edge of the formation. It was mildly maneuvering, and the Japanese rear gunner was squirting away as I came down from behind. I worked in close, gave him a burst, and set the plane afire quickly. The Judy headed for the water, trailing a long plume of smoke. I pulled up again to find two more Judys flying a loose wing. I came in from the rear to send one of them down burning. Dipping my Hellcat's wing, I slid over onto the other and got it on the same pass. It caught fire also, and I could see the rear gunner continuing to pepper away at me as he disappeared in an increasingly sharp arc downward. For a split second I almost felt sorry for the little bastard.

That made three down, and we were now getting close to our fleet. Though the number of enemy planes had been pretty

Admiral Chester Nimitz (left) discusses strategy with a fellow naval officer.

well chopped down, many still remained. It did not look like we would score a grand slam, and I reported this to our flight director's office. The sky appeared full of smoke and pieces of aircraft, as we tried to ride herd on the remaining enemy planes in an effort to keep them from scattering.

Another meatball broke formation ahead and I slid onto his tail, again working in close, due a great deal to my inability to see clearly through my oil-smeared windshield. I gave him a short burst, but it was enough. The rounds went right into the sweet spot at the root of his wing. Other rounds must have hit the pilot or control cables, as the burning plane twisted crazily out of control.

Despite our efforts, the Jills started their descent for their torpedo runs and the remaining Judys prepared to peel off for their bombing runs. I headed for a group of three Judys flying in a long column. By the time I had reached the tail-ender, we were almost over our outer screen of ships, but still fairly high when the first Judy was about to begin his dive. As he started his nose-over, I noticed a black puff that appeared beside him in the sky—our five-inch guns were beginning to open up.

Trying to disregard the flak, I overtook the nearest bomber. It seemed that I had scarcely touched the gun trigger when his engine began to come to pieces. The Judy started smoking, then torching on-and-off, as it disappeared below me. The next plane was about one-fifth of the way down in his dive before I caught up with him. This time

a short burst produced astonishing results. Number six blew up with a tremendous explosion, right in my face. I must have hit his bomb. I have seen planes blow up before, but never like this! I yanked the stick up sharply to avoid the scattered pieces and hot stuff, then radioed, "Splash number six! There's one more ahead, and he's headed for a BB (battleship). I don't think he'll make it." Hardly had the words left my mouth than the Judy caught a direct hit that removed it permanently. The pilot had apparently run into a solid curtain of steel from the battlewagon.

Looking around, it seemed that only Hellcats were in the sky with me. Glancing back along the route from where we had come, in a pattern 35 miles long, I saw flaming oil slicks in the water, and smoke still hanging in the air. It did not seem like eight minutes, but that's all it was—an eight-minute opportunity for a flight of a lifetime.

I was satisfied with the day's events and felt that I had contributed my personal payback for Pearl Harbor.

The Marines at Peleliu

On September 15, 1944, U.S. Marine and Army units invaded the island of Peleliu, one of the Palau Islands roughly six hundred miles east of the Philippines. Peleliu was to serve as a stepping stone in the campaign to retake the Philippines from the Japanese. Securing the island took over a

A U.S. Marine on Peleliu. Both U.S. and Japanese suffered heavy casualties in the battle to capture the island.

month, despite the fact that Peleliu is only about six miles long and two miles wide.

The battle was fought in tropical heat and on rugged terrain that provided the Japanese defenders with excellent cover. The marine and army units that landed on Peleliu had to claw their way forward, from foxhole to foxhole, rooting out the Japanese from their bunkers and cave complexes. More than eighteen hundred Americans died in the struggle, and another eight thousand were wounded. The Japanese lost roughly eleven thousand soldiers. E.B. Sledge was a soldier with the 1st Marine Division on Peleliu. He took notes

on the battle as it progressed and later expanded them into an autobiographical account of his time in the Pacific. Sledge writes of carnage, depression, and the ever-present specter of death that haunted the tiny island.

It is difficult to convey to anyone who has not experienced it the ghastly horror of having your sense of smell saturated constantly with the putrid odor of rotting human flesh day after day, night after night. This was something the men of an infantry battalion got a horrifying dose of during a long, protracted battle such as Peleliu. In the tropics the dead became bloated and gave off a terrific stench within a few hours after death. . . .

Each time we moved into a different position I could determine the areas occupied by each rifle company. . . . Behind each company position lay a pile of ammo and supplies and the inevitable rows of dead under their ponchos. We could determine how bad that sector of the line was by the number of dead. To see them so always filled me with anger at the war and the realization of senseless waste. It depressed me far more than my own fear. . . .

I still see clearly the landscape around one particular position we occupied for several days. It was a scene of destruction and desolation that no fiction could invent. The area was along the southwestern border of the pocket where ferocious fighting had gone on since the second day of battle (16 September). The 1st Marines, the 7th Marines, and now the 5th Marines, all in their turn, had fought against this same section of ridges. Our exhausted battalion, 3/5, moved into the line to relieve another slightly more exhausted battalion. It was the same old weary shuffling of one tired, depleted outfit into the line to relieve another whose sweating men trudged out of their positions, hollow-eyed, stooped, grimy, bearded zombies.

The Company K riflemen and machine gunners climbed up the steep ridge and into the crevices and holes of the company we relieved. Orders were given that no one must look over the crest of the ridge, because enemy rifle and machine-gun fire would kill instantly anyone who did.

As usual the troops pulling out gave our men "the dope" on the local conditions: what type of fire to expect, particular danger spots and possible infiltration routes at night. . . .

When . . . we came closer to the gun pit to set up our mortar, I saw [that the pit's] white coral sides and bottom were spattered and smeared with the dark red blood of . . . two comrades.

After we got our gun emplaced, I collected up some large scraps of cardboard from ration and ammo boxes and used them to cover the bottom of the pit as well as I could. Fat, lazy blowflies were reluctant to leave the blood-smeared rock.

I had long since become used to the sight of blood, but the idea of sitting in that bloodstained gun pit was a bit too much for me. It seemed almost like leaving our dead unburied to sit on the blood of a fellow Marine spilled out on the coral. . . . As I looked at the stains . . . I recalled some of the eloquent phrases of politicians and newsmen about how "gallant" it is for a man to "shed his blood for his country," and "to give his life's blood as a sacrifice," and so on. The words seemed so ridiculous. Only the flies benefited.

Excerpted from *With Old Breed at Peleliu and Okinawa*, by E.B. Sledge (Novata, CA: Presidio Press, 1981. Copyright © 1981 by E.B. Sledge. Reprinted with permission.

VE Day on Okinawa

While people in the United States celebrated Victory in Europe Day on May 8, 1945, American soldiers were still fighting and dying in the Pacific. U.S. troops had invaded the Japanese home islands in early 1945—Iwo Jima in February and Okinawa in April. When news of the German surrender came, the bloody fight for Okinawa was not even half over. Gordon Cobbledick sent a radio dispatch from Okinawa to the Cleveland Plain Dealer *on May 8, reminding the newspaper's readers that the struggle against fascist tyranny did not end with the fall of the Third Reich. It would be three more months—and thousands of more casualties—before Imperial Japan would surrender.*

Okinawa, May 8 (Via Navy Radio)—We stood in the rain this morning and heard the voice from San Francisco, only half believing. There had been so many false reports. But this seemed to be the McCoy [the real thing].

"Confirmed by Gen. Eisenhower's headquarters," the voice was saying. "Prime Minister Churchill proclaimed May 8 as V-E Day."

Artillery thundered and the planes roared low overhead and we couldn't hear all that the voice was saying.

"President Truman . . . Marshal Stalin announced . . . the Canadian government

A U.S. marine on Okinawa. Even after the Allies won the war in Europe, fighting continued in the Pacific.

at Ottawa . . . unauthorized announcement . . . American news agency . . ."

So this was V-E Day. It was V-E Day in the United States and Great Britain and Russia, but on Okinawa the ambulances skidded through the sticky red mud and bounced over rutted, rocky coral roads. Some of the men who rode them gritted their teeth behind bloodless lips and let no cry escape them. Some stared skyward through eyes that were dull with the look of men to whom nothing mattered greatly. Some screamed with pain that the morphine couldn't still. And some lay very quiet under ponchos that covered their faces.

It was V-E Day all over the world, but on Okinawa two doughboys lay flat behind a jagged rock and one said, "I know where the bastard is and I'm going to get him."

He raised his head and looked and then he stood, half crouched, and brought his Garand into position.

When he tumbled backward the rifle clattered on the rocks. The boy looked up and smiled sheepishly and said, "I hurt my arm when I fell," and the blood gushed

A U.S. marine takes aim at a Japanese sniper on Okinawa.

from his mouth and ran in a quick torrent over the stubble of beard on his young face, and he was dead.

It was V-E Day at home, but on Okinawa men shivered in fox holes half filled with water and waited for the command to move forward across the little green valley that was raked from both ends by machine-gun fire.

It was V-E Day, but on Okinawa a staff officer sat looking dully at the damp earthen floor of his tent. A young lieutenant, his green field uniform plastered with mud, stood awkwardly beside him.

"I was with him, sir," the lieutenant said. "It was a machine-gun bullet, sir. He never knew what hit him." He paused. "He was a good marine, sir."

The staff officer said, "He was the only son we had."

On Okinawa a flame-throwing tank lumbered across a narrow plain toward an enemy pillbox. From a cave a gun spat viciously and the tank stopped and burst into fire. When the crewmen clambered out machine guns chattered and they fell face forward in the mud and were still.

It was V-E Day everywhere, but on Okinawa the forests of white crosses grew and boys who had hardly begun to live died miserably in the red clay of this hostile land.

It was a day of celebration, but on Okinawa the war moved on. Not swiftly, for swift war cannot be waged against an enemy who burrows underground where bombs and shells and all the instruments of quick destruction can't touch him. Not gloriously, for there is little glory in any war and none

at all in cold and mud. But the enemy wouldn't wait and the war moved on.

It was V-E Day, and on Okinawa a soldier asked, "What are they going to do back in the States—get drunk and forget about us out here?"

Another said, "So they'll open the race tracks and turn on the lights and give people all the gas they want and the hell with us."

Another said, "They'll think the war is over and they'll quit their jobs and leave us to fight these bastards with pocket knives."

You told them it wasn't so. You said the people would have their day of celebration and then would go grimly back to the job of producing what is needed so desperately out here.

And you hoped to God that what you were saying was the truth.

Excerpted from ""Japanese Steel on Okinawa," by Gordon Cobbledick, *Cleveland Plain Dealer*, May 8, 1945. Copyright © 1945 by Gordon Cobbledick. Reprinted with permission.

The Decision to Use the Bomb

In July 1945, President Harry S. Truman was attending a conference in Potsdam, Germany, with British prime minister Winston Churchill and Soviet leader Josef Stalin. The subject of their meeting was the restructuring of Europe after Germany's surrender. It was during this meeting that the president received word from Secretary of War Henry Stimson that tests of the new atomic bomb had been successful. Since the Allies were still at war with Japan, Truman was faced with the decision of what to do with this

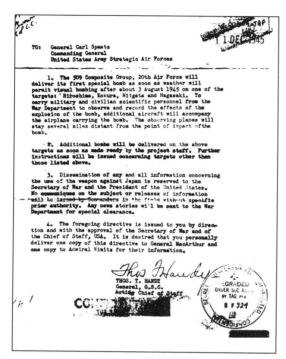

A facsimile of the document authorizing the U.S. military to drop the atomic bomb on Japan in 1945.

awesome weapon. American forces were poised to invade the larger home islands of Japan, but past island invasions against the Japanese had taught the president and his advisers that the cost in American lives would be staggering.

Under much advisement, Truman eventually ordered the dropping of two atomic bombs on Japan—the first on Hiroshima, and when that failed to prompt immediate surrender, a second on Nagasaki. In Truman's memoirs, he recalls how he made the decision that led to the destruction of these two cities and the end of World War II.

If the test of the bomb was successful, I wanted to afford Japan a clear chance to end the fighting before we made use of this newly gained power. If the test should fail, then it would be even more important to us to bring about a surrender before we had to make a physical conquest of Japan. [Chief of staff of the army] General [George C.] Marshall told me that it might cost half a million American lives to force the enemy's surrender on his home grounds.

But the test was now successful. The entire development of the atomic bomb had been dictated by military considerations. The idea of the atomic bomb had been suggested to President [Franklin D.] Roosevelt by the famous and brilliant Dr. Albert Einstein, and its development turned out to be a vast undertaking. It was the achievement of the combined efforts of science, industry, labor, and the military, and it had no parallel in history. . . .

[Secretary Stimson suggested] that I had then set up a committee of top men and had asked them to study with great care the implications the new weapon might have for us. . . .

This committee was assisted by a group of scientists . . . [that included] Dr. Oppenheimer, Dr. Arthur H. Compton, Dr. E.O. Lawrence, and the Italian-born Dr. Enrico Fermi. . . .

It was their recommendation that the bomb be used against the enemy as soon as it could be done. They recommended further that it should be used without specific warning and against a target that would clearly show its devastating strength. . . . It was their conclusion that no technical demonstration they might propose, such as over a deserted island, would be likely to bring the war to an end. . . .

The final decision of where and when to use the atomic bomb was up to me. Let there be no mistake about it. I regarded the bomb as a military weapon and never had any doubt that it should be used. The top military advisors to the President recommended its use, and when I talked to Churchill he unhesitatingly told me that he favored the use of the atomic bomb if it might aid to end the war.

In deciding to use this bomb I wanted to make sure that it would be used as a weapon of war in the manner prescribed by the laws of war. That meant that I wanted it dropped on a military target. I had told Stimson that

Franklin D. Roosevelt (left) and Harry S. Truman. The secret development of the atomic bomb began during Roosevelt's term in office.

the bomb should be dropped as nearly as possible upon a war production center of prime military importance. . . .

Four cities were finally recommended as targets: Hiroshima, Kokura, Niigata, and Nagasaki. They were listed in that order as targets for the first attack. . . .

On July 28 Radio Tokyo announced that the Japanese government would continue to fight. . . . There was no alternative now. The bomb was scheduled to be dropped after August 3 unless Japan surrendered before that day.

On August 6, the fourth day of the journey home from Potsdam, came the historic news that shook the world.

Excerpted from *Memoirs by Harry S. Truman, Volume 1: Year of Decisions*, by Harry S. Truman (Garden City, NY: Doubleday, 1955). Copyright © 1955 by Doubleday. Reprinted with permission.

VJ Day

With two of the nation's cities devastated by nuclear blasts and an invasion of the home islands imminent, the Japanese government surrendered on August 15, 1945. Despite protests from proud military leaders, the Japanese Emperor made the difficult announcement that Japan would surrender unconditionally to the Allies. American general Douglas MacArthur was appointed Supreme Allied Commander and given the task of receiving the Japanese surrender. In Tokyo Bay, aboard the battleship USS Missouri, *MacArthur witnessed the signing of the surrender documents on September 2. The Japanese foreign minister, Mamoru Shigemitsu, and the chief of the imperial staff, Yoshijiro Umeza, represented Japan. After they signed the terms, representatives of the Allied nations added their signatures. MacArthur closed the proceedings by affixing his name last.*

In the United States, President Harry S. Truman made an official announcement on September 2 regarding the historic significance of Victory over Japan Day. Trumans' message emphasized the triumph of democracy over tyranny. He pointed toward the future and insisted that America become an example for peace and international goodwill. The United States, of course, had escaped the war relatively unscathed, but Japan—and indeed much of the rest of the world—was now faced with the task of rebuilding their countries after the long, divisive, and destructive conflict.

My fellow Americans, the thoughts and hopes of all America—indeed of all the civilized world—are centered tonight on the battleship *Missouri*. There on that small piece of American soil anchored in Tokyo Harbor the Japanese have just officially laid down their arms. They have signed terms of an unconditional surrender.

Four years ago the thoughts and fears of the whole civilized world were centered on another piece of American soil—Pearl Harbor. The mighty threat to civilization which began there is now laid to rest. It was a long road to Tokyo—and a bloody one.

We shall not forget Pearl Harbor.

The Japanese militarists will not forget the USS *Missouri*.

The evil done by the Japanese war lords can never be repaired or forgotten. But their power to destroy and kill has been

A jubilant crowd in San Francisco celebrates Japan's surrender on August 15, 1945.

taken from them. Their armies and what is left of their navy are now impotent.

To all of us there comes first a sense of gratitude to Almighty God who sustained us and our Allies in the dark days of grave danger, who made us . . . grow from weakness into the strongest fighting force in history, and who now has seen us overcome the forces of tyranny that sought to destroy His civilization. . . .

Our first thoughts, of course—thoughts of gratefulness and deep obligation—go out to those of our loved ones who have been killed or maimed in this terrible war. On land and sea and in the air, American men and women have given their lives so that this day of ultimate victory might come and assure the survival of a civilized world. . . .

We think of those whom death in this war has hurt, taking from them husbands, sons, brothers and sisters whom they loved. No victory can bring back the faces they longed to see.

Only the knowledge that the victory, which these sacrifices made possible, will be wisely used can give them any comfort. It is our responsibility—ours, the living—to see to it that this victory shall be a monument worthy of the dead who died to win it. . . .

This is a victory of more than arms alone. This is a victory of liberty over tyranny.

Japanese and American representatives meet to sign surrender documents on September 2, 1945.

From our war plants rolled the tanks and planes which blasted their way to the heart of our enemies; from our shipyards sprang the ships which bridged all the oceans of the world for our weapons and supplies; from our farms came the food and fibre for our armies and navies and for our Allies in all the corners of the earth; from our mines and factories came the raw materials and the finished products which gave us the equipment to overcome our enemies.

But back of it all were the will and spirit and determination of a free people—who know what freedom is, and who know that it is worth whatever price they had to pay to preserve it.

It was the spirit of liberty which gave us our armed strength and which made our men invincible in battle. We now know that that spirit of liberty, the freedom of the individual, and the personal dignity of man are the strongest and toughest and most enduring forces in the world.

And so on V-J Day, we take renewed faith and pride in our own way of life. We have had our day of rejoicing over this victory. We have had our day of prayer and devotion. Now let us set aside V-J Day as one of renewed consecration to the principles which have made us the strongest nation on earth and which, in this war, we have striven so mightily to preserve. . . .

We face the future and all its dangers with great confidence and great hope. America can build for itself a future of employment and security. Together with the United Nations, it can build a world of peace founded on justice and fair dealing and tolerance. . . .

From this day we move forward. We move toward a new era of security at home. With the other United Nations we move toward a new and better world of peace and international goodwill and cooperation.

God's help has brought us to this day of victory. With His help we will attain that peace and prosperity for ourselves and all the world in the years ahead.

★ Chronology of Events ★

September 1, 1939

Germany invades Poland. France and Britain ally with Poland and declare war on Germany.

September 5, 1939

President Roosevelt proclaims U.S. neutrality.

November 4, 1939

Roosevelt amends the Neutrality Act to allow Allied nations to buy war materials from the United States.

June 22, 1940

France surrenders to Germany after roughly a month of fighting. Britain stands alone against the Third Reich.

September 16, 1940

Roosevelt institutes a military draft.

March 11, 1941

The United States begins the Lend-Lease program to aid Britain.

June 22, 1941

Germany invades the Soviet Union, opening a costly second front and casting aside its plans to invade England.

July 25, 1941

In response to Japanese aggression in Indochina, Roosevelt calls for the freezing of all Japanese assets in the United States.

December 7, 1941

Japan stages a surprise attack on the U.S. Pacific fleet stationed at Pearl Harbor, Hawaii. The following day, America declares war on Japan.

December 11, 1941

Germany and Italy, supporting Japan, declare war on the United States.

February 19, 1942

Roosevelt issues Executive Order 9066, giving the government the power to round up Japanese Americans. One hundred and twenty thousand Japanese Americans from Oregon, Washington, and California are placed in internment camps.

April 9, 1942

Japanese ground forces capture a large American army trapped on the Bataan Peninsula of the Philippine island of Luzon. General Douglas MacArthur escapes the fate of his penned up army and vows to return to liberate the island nation.

June 4, 1942

The Japanese are soundly defeated at Midway Island and the Americans seize the initiative.

August 7, 1942

The United States launches its first major offensive in the Pacific, landing marines at Guadalcanal.

November 8, 1942

Operation Torch begins as American troops and other allies overcome French colonial forces in North Africa.

April 1943

America begins the design and testing of atomic weapons at Los Alamos, New Mexico.

May 11, 1943

An American troop convoy lands at Attu, a small Aleutian island taken by the Japanese in 1942. The island will not be secured until May 30.

July 10, 1943

Allied armies invade Sicily. Italian dictator Benito Mussolini's government falls.

September 8, 1943

The new Italian government declares that it surrenders to the Allies. German forces in Italy, however, are determined to fight.

September 9, 1943

American forces land at Salerno, Italy, and begin the fight for the Italian mainland.

November 28–December 1, 1943

The "Big Three"—Roosevelt, Churchill, and Stalin—meet at Tehran, Iran.

June 6, 1944

Operation Overlord commences as Allied armies invade Normandy, France. From the small beachheads, the Allies begin the liberation of Western Europe.

June 15, 1944

An American assault convoy lands at Saipan.

August 25, 1944

German forces evacuate Paris and regroup in eastern France.

October 20, 1944

U.S. Marines stage an amphibious assault on the Philippines island of Leyte. The liberation of the Philippines begins.

December 12, 1944

The German military launches a desperate counterattack in the Ardennes region of Belgium.

January 20, 1945

Nearly all Japanese Americans held in relocation camps are permitted to return home. Most find their old jobs, farms, and houses taken by new residents.

March 8–19, 1945

The Allies capture an intact bridge at Remagen, Germany. The bridge allows the Allies to cross the Rhine—the last defensive barrier in the west—and advance into the German heartland.

April 1945

Allied armies liberate Nazi concentration camps.

April 1, 1945

American forces invade Okinawa, a small island very close to the Japanese home islands.

April 12, 1945

Roosevelt dies and Vice President Harry S. Truman assumes the presidency.

April 30, 1945

Adolf Hitler commits suicide.

May 7, 1945

The German command surrenders to the Allies.

May 8, 1945

Allies celebrate Victory in Europe Day.

August 6, 1945

The first atom bomb is dropped on Hiroshima, Japan. Three days later, a second will be dropped on Nagasaki and Japan will sue for peace.

August 15, 1945

The Allies celebrate Victory over Japan Day.

September 2, 1945

Japanese delegates sign the official terms of surrender aboard the battleship *Missouri*.

☆ Index ☆

★ Picture Credits ★

★ About the Editor ★

Author David M. Haugen edits books for Lucent Books and Greenhaven Press. He holds a master's degree in English literature and has also worked as a writer and instructor.